Realistic Model Railroad
DESIGN

Your step-by-step guide to creating a unique operating layout

Tony Koester

Photos by the author unless otherwise noted

KALMBACH
BOOKS

Printed in Canada

06 07 08 09 10 11 12 13   10 9 8 7 6 5 4 3 2

Visit our Web site at
http://kalmbachbooks.com
Secure online ordering available

Publisher's Cataloging-in-Publication
(Provided by Quality Books, Inc.)

Koester, Tony.
    Realistic model railroad design / Tony Koester.
    p. cm.
    Includes index.
    ISBN 0-89024-581-9

    1. Railroads—Models—Design and construction.
I. Title.

TF197.K585 2004   625.1'9
                            QBI04-200028

ISBN-10: 0-89024-581-9
ISBN-13: 978-0-89024-581-1

Art director: Kristi Ludwig
Book design: Sabine Beaupré

Cover photo: Jim Forbes

Contents

Introduction

This evocative foggy-morning portrait of mountain railroading by W. Allen McClelland tells everything one needs to know: the railroad's identity and approximate era (the caboose is painted in the Virginian & Ohio's post-merger Appalachian Lines scheme; the F40PH on Amtrak's *Ridge Runner* evokes the '70s), its location (central Appalachian coal country), its scope (a reasonably profitable class-one railroad, as evidenced by good ballast and a freshly painted caboose of recent vintage, even on this eastbound local), and the season (a muggy summer day). There's nothing implausible here to detract from this snapshot of a successful railroad going about its daily business.

There's so much more to "designing a model railroad" than arranging benchwork and track. Where is the prototype or type of railroad on which it's based located? Where does it go? What sort of traffic operates on its rails? Does it intersect with other lines? What period does the model railroad represent? Is it a big-time operation that could afford the very best, or some hand-me-down short line that barely made its payroll each week?

My first book, *Realistic Model Railroad Operation* (Kalmbach, 2003), focused on giving your trains a realistic, interesting purpose to match their prototypical appearance. This companion book will help you put that operation into context.

I don't believe that we can realize the full value of even a superbly crafted model unless we put it through its paces in a manner that replicates what its prototype does or did for a living—this is not a hobby primarily about displaying models on a mantelpiece. By the same token, operating sessions are more realistic and satisfying if the overall appearance is in harmony with the action.

It follows that a 1957 Chevy hardtop will glare back at the viewer in a 1940s scene, and a Burlington Northern Santa Fe Dash 9 is way out of its depth in a 1960s scene. The old saw about model railroading— "It's my railroad, so I can do anything I want"—should be checked at the door for our purposes. True as that adage is, communication may suffer if your layout doesn't make sense to others. If the people helping you build or operate your layout can't understand its parameters and goals, they will be hard-pressed to share its rewards.

No matter how complete and detailed your railroad may become, it can't handle all the communications chores on its own. People bring a wealth of experiences to the table when they visit a model railroad, and those impressions affect what they see. Almost anything that's out of place will catch the eye and sound a discordant note. It may be a little thing, like a red stop sign or a red, white, and blue mailbox in the steam era. Or a big thing, like a freelanced paint scheme on a new EMD F3 that doesn't look like someone at EMD drew it.

The purpose of *Realistic Model Railroad Design* is to help you understand the fundamentals that underlie a successful model railroad as judged by an audience of knowledgeable observers.

Important as your own goals and opinions may be, unless they fit into a reality understood and largely determined by others, your layout may fall short of the mark. If together we can reduce the number of times you are prompted to mutter, "Um, I can explain that," this book will have succeeded.

What follows is an assemblage of facts, concepts, and opinions that you may want to consider as you formulate and review your model railroad design criteria. As you do so, ask how they measure up against those used by modelers who are highly regarded by their peers and consider whether that's important to you now or may become so in the future.

This means that I have walked squarely into the crosshairs, as many of the illustrations in this book are of my former HO model railroad, the Allegheny Midland. At this juncture several years after dismantling that railroad to make way for what is becoming an even more fulfilling layout, however, I have a clear perspective not only of what I did right but where I came up short.

I'll share both my "atta boys" and my "nice tries" with you in the hopes that you can do a better job than I did. We'll look at many aspects of the "Midland Road"—from its name and nickname to its herald, paint scheme, locale, era, roster, prototype versus freelanced theme, and primary sources of traffic— and compare them to what I believe are reasonable criteria for modelers to aspire to in the 21st century.

One last thought: This book is not intended as a checklist of things that you must do to ensure that your next model railroad will be a crowning success. There are many paths to success based on personal preferences, so only some of the lessons of this book will apply to your objectives. My goal is to enhance your awareness of model railroad design opportunities without unduly constraining your creativity.

Enjoy!

CHAPTER ONE

Freelancing within limits

Fig. 1-1: Freelancing within the guidelines furnished by base prototypes—the approach called "prototype-based freelancing"—was the method followed to create the HO scale Allegheny Midland layout referenced here. Parent Nickel Plate Road equipment was freely intermixed, as shown by the two lead units on the coal drag.

In model railroad terms, "freelancing" means designing a layout that isn't based on a specific actual railroad, called a "prototype." Freelancing may perhaps be too broad an approach for the purposes of this book. We can't assume that "anything goes" when the aim is a realistic appearance or operating scheme. I therefore recommend that freelancers situate their railroads in time and space, and give them plausible names and paint schemes to help viewers understand their era, locale, and mission. We should look for creative ways to ease the communication needs that are a part of any successful layout as we share our goals and accomplishments with others.

Fig. 1-2: Prototypes might include the "European-style" ziggerat architecture commonly seen in some regions of North America. The Claremont & Concord used to run down this street.

Prototype or freelanced?

I don't intend to take sides in the debate about whether it's better, or trendier, to model a specific prototype than it is to freelance. I spent 25 years planning, designing, building, and operating a freelanced model railroad (fig. 1-1) and enjoyed that process thoroughly. I know, too, that a mythical railroad can be plausible enough that observers come to regard it as a prototype in its own right.

Conversely, I am now enjoying the chance to re-create in miniature a portion of a long-time favorite: the Nickel Plate Road, including scenes in the Indiana town where I spent much of my youth (fig. 11-3). I've found this experience dramatically different from freelancing—yet not necessarily better.

In this chapter I will look at the opportunities and challenges of the freelancer, then consider the potential of prototype modeling.

Challenges of freelancing

The dean of track planners, the late John Armstrong, was well known as the architect of the O scale Canandaigua Southern. The CS was a freelanced railroad, so John spoke from experience when he stated that coming up with a plausible concept for a freelanced railroad and executing it well is harder than designing an equally good prototype model.

John's premise was that a prototype modeler has clear benchmarks against which to measure success. Paint a Baltimore & Ohio Geep or F unit the wrong shade of blue and it will stand out like a dandelion on a putting green. But how do we measure the "quality" of a freelanced paint scheme or structure? What pulls the parts into a cohesive whole?

As it turns out, evaluating freelanced paint schemes on most first-generation diesels is remarkably easy, as I'll discuss in chapter 5. Each major builder's diesel liveries usually had a distinctive flavor that displayed traits of only a few graphic designers.

Similarly, architecture tends to be regional. Many older commercial structures in eastern cities, for example, reflect the European heritage of the immigrants who designed and built them (fig. 1-2). This makes adapting commercial kits of European heritage for North American usage not too difficult, although they're not suitable for all parts of the continent. The main feature of European structure kits that will need alteration is the distinctive window glazing pattern of a large single pane below with two smaller ones above. In North America—

with the primary exception of the Province of Quebec with its many structures of French heritage—windows tend to be divided in half.

Many of the commercial structure kits are freelanced. This approach differs from that of selective compression, where a modeler reduces all dimensions to allow a huge prototype structure to fit into a typical model railroad scene without losing the visual characteristics of the original. My guess is that many who manufacture such kits enjoy demonstrating their skill as architects-in-miniature, while many modelers appreciate the more fanciful or ornate look that results.

Model rule, not exception

The look of the railroad in the region and the era being depicted guides a prototype modeler. A freelancer, on the other hand, needs to look around the region he or she plans to model to discover what is typical without being unduly influenced by the eye-catching exceptions. A typical general observation might be that white-painted structures predominate in many areas of North America in the mid-20th century (fig. 1-3). Residences

and businesses made of brick or those painted in a color typically feature white trim. The trim on brick industrial buildings, however, might be painted green, black, or gray as an alternative to white.

The complete scene

Some modelers focus on a handful of key structures rather than the complete scene. When doing so, they build layouts that tend to look more like showcases of architectural oddities than scenes that look familiar and ordinary. This may be by design. After all, who needs more "ordinary" than we face each day?

Like many other modelers, however, I've found that a lot of ordinary can add up to something extraordinary. If a scene looks right, which is to say it looks like what we expect to see, it looks realistic. But if it looks like an idyllic painting with the blemishes edited out, it will fail to convince us that all is well. All may be pretty and pert and factory-new, but that's not how the real world looks. Modelers who present a squeaky-clean Disneyland in lieu of reality may regret that choice when the time comes to share their efforts.

Fig. 1-3: In the 1960s, one persuasive siding salesman could standardize the look of a entire company town, transforming it into a collection of colorful frame structures trimmed in white.

Except for mantelpiece models, which are often assumed to be the equivalent of a full-sized locomotive or car viewed in the artificial context of a museum, the reality of a model is tied to the perception of the viewer. Our task is to fool that viewer into thinking of the model in a real-world setting by showing convincing details: faded paint, exhaust residue, oxidized metal, hard-water deposits running down boiler jacketing, mud splashed up from grade crossings and dirty ballast, grease drips, and oil marks from parts that spin and reciprocate (fig. 1-4).

The viewer probably knows what a Burlington F unit or Geep looks like. Consciously or subconsciously, that knowledge of the prototype overlays any model. If it looks like the Burlington and operates like the Burlington, it must be the Burlington.

A coherent story

Without a base prototype, a freelancer has no such point of reference. That we admire many freelanced railroads often is the result of their builders' abilities to tell a coherent story.

Model the Monon and you know at once what types of locomotives it had, when its first F3 or Century 628 was acquired and last traded in, how the railroad painted and lettered its cabooses, and when the railroad merged into the Louisville & Nashville (part of CSX today). But what diesels did the freelanced Virginian & Ohio use to vanquish steam? How were they painted? What steam types did they replace? When did second-generation units show up? What were they? How did the paint schemes differ? Rewarding as it is to resolve decisions like these, pitfalls lie at every turn.

Allen McClelland never

designed the as-delivered paint scheme for the V&O "covered wagons" until he did so as an exercise for this book (chapter 5). He hadn't created that paint scheme in 1958 when he was designing and building the original Afton Division layout because, at that time, many full-sized railroads were simplifying their paint schemes. Intricate ideas demand more time at the workbench unless you start with a prototypical scheme and slightly modify it. So Allen adopted a "dip blue" scheme that looked right for the era he was modeling; change V&O blue to black and you almost replicate the Clinchfield's scheme (fig. 1-5). That's good because, like the CRR, the V&O is an Appalachian coal hauler.

Allen's perceptiveness saved him time at a critical

Fig. 1-4: Weathering puts models into a context by establishing usage, age, and environment. Here a V&O SD24 in its as-delivered paint scheme leads a U25C that was repainted in the color scheme adopted just prior to the Appalachian Lines merger that occurred in 1968.

Fig. 1-5: In the '60s, many railroads switched to more austere paint colors. For example, the Clinchfield dropped its distinctive gray-and-yellow livery, seen on the GP38 at right, for all-black. The V&O followed suit with an all-blue color scheme.

juncture, without venturing into pure freelancing. Moreover, like common white frame structures, the blandness of the V&O diesel scheme helped unify the railroad. Imagine how much more attention-getting his diesels could have been had he painted them yellow or red? But that would have been counterproductive. Allen wanted visitors and operators to focus on the V&O as a vital link in North America's transportation network, not as an example of his modeling prowess.

Don't think of Allen's simplified paint schemes or, in a broader context, his well-known "good enough" philosophy as a cover-up for a lack of modeling skills. He has scratchbuilt many blue-ribbon-winning models. But none of them are the type that you'll see pictured on the boxes for the better craftsman kits. Few of those would have been appropriate for the V&O's central Appalachian locale. It's the railroad and its setting as a whole, not the pieces, that make the freelanced V&O plausible and successful.

"Prototype-based freelancing"

Several decades ago, I coined the term "prototype-based freelancing" to describe a freelanced railroad that is closely based on a specific prototype or several related prototypes. It's an imperfect but useful term for modelers who establish easily understood parameters for their freelancing endeavors.

My Allegheny Midland RR offered a reasonable example of how the process works. The name did not clearly relate it to any full-sized railroad, but it did locate the railroad within a specific region. The nickname, the Midland Road, tied the layout

Fig. 1-6: Allegheny Midland equipment was painted to match the parent company NKP's specifications. At a glance, little differentiates the two hoppers. The caboose also mimics a NKP prototype.

Fig. 1-7: Prototype free-lancers can often save time by using models painted for their base prototype and replacing the road number and name, as the author did on this Nickel Plate Road Fairbanks-Morse H-10-44 switcher from Walthers.

closer to its assumed parent railroad, the Nickel Plate Road. Indeed, the equipment was painted almost exactly like the NKP's save for the substitution of "Midland" for "Nickel Plate" and "AM" for "NKP" (fig. 1-6).

"Why not just model the NKP and be done with it?" friends used to ask. I wanted to place the railroad in West Virginia and Virginia to model the spectacular yet manageable Appalachian scenery and to create an interchange with my friend Allen McClelland's Virginian & Ohio.

Prototype-based freelancing allows you to use factory-painted models of the base prototype's locomotives and rolling stock, substituting your slightly modified road

name and perhaps changing the numbers (fig. 1-7). You may be able to use commercial decal sets for striping and other graphic elements and pre-mixed paint for the locomotive and cars. This helps the finished model look familiar and more realistic.

What you may lose in the process is a sense of "owning" the paint scheme. I initially thought I should make my own mark on the AM's graphics standards, but in the long run my interest in the NKP proved of even greater importance. I therefore advise you to think about your priorities before settling on a paint scheme and roster.

If you choose a path that leads to greater freelancing independence than the one I selected, you need to

understand that few railroads designed first-generation diesel paint schemes, as will be discussed in chapter 5.

One last point about prototype-based freelancing: A freelanced model railroad is less believable without ties to other railroads. It helps to see freight cars lettered for the Union Pacific and Boston & Maine and Florida East Coast in freelanced trains. But when freelanced rolling stock blends to the point that it seems to be "prototype" equipment, you often enhance its realism.

Slim-gauge modeling

Decades ago, those who aimed to model the relatively obscure but ever-fascinating Maine two-foot-gauge railroads discovered a

shortcut. Acknowledging that a major manufacturer would be unlikely to produce a line of two-foot-gauge models, especially in HO (HOn2), they substituted N gauge track, trucks, and locomotive mechanisms in the HO scale setting. In HO, N gauge measures about 30″ between the rails; they deemed that close enough to the desired 24″ gauge. This allowed Maine two-footers to be convincingly modeled, on a budget and without the use of scratchbuilt trucks and mechanisms.

From the outset, two of the leading proponents of HOn2½ modeling were Dave Frary and Bob Hayden. Their efforts to establish the freelanced Carrabasset & Dead River

as a plausible railroad have succeeded (fig. 1-8). The name, gauge, and scenery help place their mythical railroad "Down East."

More recently, Bachmann has produced a variety of steam locomotives and rolling stock built to O (¼″) scale but running on HO gauge track, or On2½. I've seen many portable layout sections built in this scale and gauge, which offers a relatively inexpensive way to model narrow gauge in a more robust size. On2½ is bound to gain in popularity for several reasons: low cost; the large size of the models that can still fit into a space normally used for HO; and the obvious allure of narrow-gauge railroading. That On3 modelers have the capacity to use the models by changing the gauge also helps sales.

HOn2½ and On2½ (fig. 1-9) offer great places for freelancers to get started in or return to model railroading. They may find, as Dave and Bob have, that these sizes offer everything needed for a lifetime of hobby fun.

If you've taken a cruise in Alaska, you've probably been on the famous White Pass & Yukon, a three-foot-gauge railroad that provided freight service from the port at

Skagway up into the Yukon province of Canada well into the diesel era. The WP&Y bought a variety of Alco and GE diesels, and its Alco DL-535Es (fig. 1-10) looked like the modern Century-series standard-gauge hood units. LGB offers the 535 in G (1:22.5) scale.

The White Pass & Yukon, an interesting railroad by anyone's measure, offers intriguing possibilities for prototype modelers and, I think, for freelancers. Remove some of the winterizing details from the LGB DL-535E and you have a unit that could have

dieselized the East Broad Top or East Tennessee & Western North Carolina. If the EBT or ET&WNC had operated a decade or so longer into the '60s, DL-535s could have taken over. Seeing those units painted black with orange safety stripes and EBT lettering

Fig. 1-9: Running On2½ quarter-inch scale models on HO gauge track and mechanisms has become a popular approach to narrow-gauge modeling with lots of room for creativity. Bill and Mary Miller run both On2½ (top) and On3 railroads in this Colorado setting.

or in Southern green lettered for the ET would be a treat.

Such revisionist history isn't much of a stretch for EBT fans, as the railroad had one huge advantage over most narrow-gauge lines: The bulk of its traffic was coal, and run-of-mine coal had to be dumped and cleaned at a preparation plant in Mount Union, Pennsylvania, before being reloaded into standard-gauge hoppers for shipment over the Pennsy. No need to make a costly and time-consuming shift of cargo from narrow- to standard-gauge cars.

The EBT also perfected a way to avoid off-loading inbound standard-gauge cars into narrow-gauge cars—called "breaking bulk"—by lifting one end of a car at a time with an overhead crane, replacing standard-gauge with narrow-gauge trucks, and hauling the car to its destination anywhere on the northern part of the railroad. This can be readily modeled, especially in a larger scale.

Extended time lines

The late Glenn Pizer, who founded the Nickel Plate Road Historical & Technical Society with me in 1966, built some models depicting the NKP as an independent road years after its 1964 merger into the Norfolk & Western. I recall an Athearn extended-vision caboose with the NKP's famous gray stripe and "High Speed Service" script slogan and an EMD SDP40 in NKP's blue-and-

Fig. 1-10: On June 20, 1972, James B. Armstrong took this photo as three units and 50 cars left Skagway, Alaska. The White Pass & Yukon was once a busy narrow-gauge railroad featuring modern diesel motive power, such as Alco (MLW) DL-535Es (right). A freelancer could build on this example by assuming that the East Broad Top (bottom) had continued freight operations into the 1960s and beyond using similar Alco or GE diesels.

aluminum passenger colors.

Assuming that a favorite railroad didn't disappear through a merger or abandonment is a valid approach to freelancing. If you find yourself attracted to Alco Century 636s or GE Dash 9s but your favorite railroad vanished years earlier, you may find that timeline extrapolation offers a reasonable solution.

Stick to your guns

When you're freelancing, friends may not be clear on the parameters of the project, so you'll get suggestions about how to "improve" the railroad. You may have decided on an all-Alco roster, only to have one kindly soul show up with a small fleet of GEs or EMDs. Next thing you know, someone else shows up with a Big Boy (on

your 1964 railroad, no less) and asks you to run his locomotive. You are now faced with the politics of layout management: Do you offend the steam guy who doesn't understand that his locomotive is from a different era? Or the diesel guy who did everything right in terms of engine type and era, but doesn't have Alcos?

Moreover, you may be urged to add jobs to keep everyone busy. That may work out, but somewhere in

this never-ending process the railroad's operating objectives will change. Your medium-density coal hauler will be running enough trains to rival the Northeast Corridor, and the aisles will remind you of a mall on Labor Day.

Take time to digest how suggested changes will affect not only the day-to-day operations and appearance of the railroad but also its—and your—long-term goals.

CHAPTER TWO

Prototype modeling

Let's face it: We're all freelancers to some degree. Nne of us has the room

to do justice to much more than a few scale miles of any railroad. Modeling an

entire division mile for mile is way beyond our means. And just because we

have locomotives and cabooses lettered for the same railroad doesn't mean

we're doing a good "prototype modeling" job of representing part of the actual

physical plant and operations of that line.

Fig. 2-1: Dan Zugelter's HO scale depiction of the Chesapeake & Ohio in the late 1940s Is remarkably realistic, as shown by these comparison photographs of the Hinton, West Virginia, engine terminal. Dan coved all of the surrounding wall and ceiling corners to ensure a seamless sky backdrop. The prototype photo is from the C&O Historical Society's archives.

Fig. 2-2: The above HO scale
model of a Chesapeake &
Ohio wooden "cabin" (seen
at left) was kitbashed from a
plastic kit for a Baltimore &
Ohio tower by using part of
each lower wall, Evergreen
styrene for the top-floor windows, and a scratchbuilt roof.

that we care about what were
once regarded as insignificant
differences between steam
locomotives (USRA light
Mikados, for example) or
diesels of the same type.

In fact, modelers in most
popular scales now have the
means to accurately model
specific prototypes within
tightly defined boundaries
of time and space. N scale
(1:160) is edging toward
HO (1:87.1) in popularity as
well as the variety and quality
of models. O scale (1:48) is
making a popular comeback
with solid support from the
leading manufacturers.

S scale (1:64) also has a
good following, especially in
Sn3, because a $^3/_{16}$"-scale,
narrow-gauge layout is not
only a nice size to view and
work on, but it fits into about
the same space as a standard-
gauge HO railroad. Outdoor

A growing trend

Let's not beg the question
by suggesting that all model
railroaders are freelancing
because no coal or oil fires
heat the water in our "steam"
locomotives' boilers or
because our "diesel-electrics"
lack internal-combustion
prime movers. Differences of
that type do not hinder our
ability to depict location (fig.
2-1), operation, and even the
sound of a given prototype.

I find modeling prototypes
different from freelancing in
many ways. For one thing, a
faithfully modeled prototype
railroad offers an increasingly
popular way to enjoy our
multi-faceted hobby. One
reason is the availability of a
wealth of information from
model railroad and railfan
magazines, railroad historical
societies, videotapes and
DVDs (often converted from
vintage 16mm films), and

resources on the Internet.

Another reason is that
many professional railroaders
are also modelers; indeed,
their interest in trains may
have led to a career in
railroading. Most of them
are eager to share what they
know, and the modeling
community has benefitted
enormously as a result.

Modelers receive incredible
support from manufacturers
and importers, who realize

"garden" railroad equipment (1:32, 1:29, 1:24, 1:22.5, and 1:20.3 scales) is being brought indoors, where it can be enjoyed year-round and detailed to a finer degree. Realistic operation is sure to follow.

Good enough

The current quest for more detailed and accurate models is compelling. If that's your thing, go for it. You'll find a sizable number of modelers who share your enthusiasm for building freight cars or diesels with exquisite detail.

But stay focused on what it requires to build a realistic model railroad. If you have no space for a layout or if you spend your summer vacation relaxing on the back porch of the family cottage, you may have the time to build up a large roster of modeling gems. If, on the other hand, you're busy building your model railroad, you may find that there's not enough time to erect the benchwork, lay and wire track, add scenery, start to operate, *and* build up a roster of contest-quality models. Not just yet, anyway.

My own situation requires that my model railroading time be spent working towards the first operating session. I may think I'm doing a fine job of building benchwork, constructing roadbed, laying track, and wiring the railroad, but I

Fig. 2-3: Tipples on the Clinchfield at Haysi (Berta), Virginia (above), and the C&O at Pikeville, Kentucky (above right), were ideal candidates for scratchbuilt tipples at Big Springs Junction, West Virginia, on the Allegheny Midland. Similar stand-in models were kitbashed in one evening using Con-Cor's Tucson Silver Mine kit and leftover parts from a Walthers coal mine (right).

won't know for sure until the gang shows up for that first session. "Oops, I'm on the ground again!" gets old fast, as does "My engine's dead!" and "I can't run around my pickup over here until you finish that crossover."

While I'm working on my railroad, I take steps to ensure that I'll have some motive power and rolling stock that are suitable for a midwestern railroad in 1954. Bill Darnaby, whose HO scale Maumee has been operating for several years, has been upgrading his freight car roster with resin kits, so I bought quite a few of his displaced cars, which have metal wheels and Kadee couplers and are nicely weathered. One day, I hope to replace those cars with better models, but for now they will do just fine. Their cost is a modest investment of cash, not time.

I have also, on occasion,

traded surplus AM models for NKP models or for decoder-installation or detailing work. Time is my most precious commodity, and I'm doing everything I can to reserve it for layout construction. Later, my focus will shift toward model building and detailing, as it

did with the AM. As I see it, the challenge is to balance saving time against "buying" my new railroad.

Sharing info and the railroad

An advantage of modeling a tightly defined prototype is that other knowledgeable modelers, railfans, and rail

Fig. 2-4: A Central Valley kit was used to build this well-detailed code 70 no. 8 turnout; nos. 5 through 9 kits for both code 70 and 83 are available. The author substituted a manganese-insert frog casting to duplicate Nickel Plate Road practice.

historians can instantly grasp what you're trying to do, and most will try to help you reach your noble objectives. Once word got around that I am now modeling the Third Subdivision of the St. Louis Division of the Clover Leaf District of the Nickel Plate Road in the fall of 1954 (that's reasonably specific, wouldn't you agree?), some modelers have walked up to me at conventions to hand me a photograph or provide information they thought I could use. Those gestures are the bedrock of this hobby.

Several of my good friends are also NKP fans and/or modelers to some extent. They regard helping with research or modeling a way to share the fun of the new layout. My good friend, civil engineer and master modeler Frank Hodina, for example, looked at an early iteration of the track plan for the new layout and said, "Let me take a crack at it." In short order, he produced a plan better than mine, with several very clever innovations.

Scratch? Or kitbash?

Much as I appreciate and can use friends' help at this juncture, I reserve many key modeling projects for myself. I look forward to scratch-building the grain elevator,

depot, and interlocking tower (fig. 11-3) in Cayuga, Indiana, my hometown during the '50s, just as I enjoyed scratchbuilding structures for the AM.

Scratchbuilding is like building a good kit, except that you don't have to bother to read the instructions. If you're concerned about your scratchbuilding skills, try a laser kit with stick-on detail parts to help you picture how such models go together, then try a simple scratch-building project like a tool or section-car house. If you use commercial styrene or wood siding materials along with fast-drying bonding agents, you can assemble these kit models almost as fast as you can cut out the parts.

Kitbashing has a place in prototype modeling. Not all models, especially those used in the background or in a busy downtown scene, need to be exact copies of their prototypes. Adjusting the details and coloration of a kit lets you capture the essence of a given prototype with a modicum of effort (fig. 2-2).

Moreover, easily built kits or built-up structures can serve as stand-ins for the scratchbuilt versions that will one day occupy the hallowed ground (fig. 2-3). You may argue the point, but I'd rather

have a reasonable facsimile of an interlocking tower at a junction in lieu of a bare spot in the scenery.

Again, don't lose sight of your original objective. The urge to build a realistic layout was powerful enough to get you started down this road. Recognize that it will be easy to check off the "build tower" box on your to-do list and then never get around to scratchbuilding the authentic model. A few stand-ins may not derail a project, but a lot of them can erode your incentive to re-create a slice of reality in a historically accurate setting. That can lead to a form of burnout.

Creative compromises

Compromises will still be needed, of course. A typical situation is my having the official NKP drawings for a no. 8 turnout, the standard size for all mainline turnouts on my layout. I planned to handlay them, as I'd done for the Allegheny Midland. Then Central Valley released a new line of nos. 5 through 9 turnout kits for code 70 or 83 rail. They're designed to AREA standards. The good news is that these kits feature details like tie plates, which I couldn't, or wouldn't, build into my handlaid versions. The bad news is that AREA

standards call for a much shorter lead—the distance between the point of the frog and the tip of the switch points—than NKP specs require. The longer lead will create a gentler curve into the diverging route, which looks better to my eye. Besides, I'm now modeling the NKP.

A reasonable compromise is to add two more ties to the CV kit, lengthening the turnout and increasing the lead. The resulting code 70 turnout (fig. 2-4) still isn't an exact copy of an NKP turnout, but it affords more detail than a handlaid one would have.

I enjoy handlaying track. Unless CV or someone else produces an equally well-detailed code 55 no. 6 or 7 turnout, I plan to handlay a lot more track. I'm using Micro Engineering's code 55 flextrack for industrial and yard trackage and code 70 on the main, but code 55 turnouts remain elusive.

Are such concerns too close to counting rivets? Not close enough? Because my objective is to model one specific segment of the NKP to the best of my ability, a compromise made today in a quest for expediency may haunt me later. After more than a quarter-century of

experience building and operating layouts, I try to anticipate which decisions will later prove to have been wise and which will eat away at my satisfaction level.

If it's something readily changed, such as dropping better freight cars onto the tracks, I'll go with the easy way for now. If it's something like a structure that can also be replaced, I'll probably use a stand-in, especially if I can readily acquire an inexpensive or quick-to-build one that will help the railroad look better. But trackwork, like benchwork and roadbed, is more permanent. In this area, I strive to come close enough to the mark to believe that I'll feel satisfied over the long haul.

Communications

Prototype modeling involves more than building accurate models. The context in which those models are displayed or operated must also match the degree of authenticity; doing otherwise would diminish the viewer's perception of its realism.

Let me cite an example. Andrew Dodge has done a remarkable job of depicting much of the narrow-gauge Denver, South Park & Pacific in the 1800s (fig. 2-5). In remote Como,

Fig. 2-5: Andrew Dodge's Denver, South Park & Pacific in On3 (circa 1882) features spectacular scenery along with challenging operations. Telephones or radios were not available, so crews use telegraph keys (above) for dispatcher communications.

Colorado, is a large open area called South Park. (The name was a good choice, since South Big Meadow doesn't have the same panache.) A stone roundhouse still stands on one side of South Park, and Andrew has re-created that structure on his On3 railroad.

Imagine the railroad's operating session. A train leaves Como and heads into the mountains. How will you tell the dispatcher when the train is at the next station? A five-channel radio set, which is fine on a modern railroad, would be out of place. Rather than allow crews to wear them, you could place those radios permanently at each station to simulate a telephone network. But the South Park didn't use phones back then either. They used telegraph to communicate. So how's your Morse code?

Andrew hedged his bet here but still came closer than most would have when attempting to simulate the

actual situation. He installed Morse-code transmitting keys at each station. Road crews use crib sheets posted by the keys to send simple reports to the dispatcher. Sending an "OS," which is the standard term used to report a train "out of station," for example, is nothing more than an O (dash-dash-dash) and an S (dot-dot-dot), as anyone who watched a movie featuring a ship in distress recalls. On the South Park, as on the ship, that would be beeeeep-beeeeep-beeeeep, beep-beep-beep.

"Beep"? Okay, Andrew cheated. It's hard to learn to use a railroad telegraph key, but the sets used to send international Morse code (versus the slightly different railroad Morse) are available.

It's also easier to understand a series of beeps in lieu of myriad relay clicks. So a dot is a beep instead of the two closely spaced clicks caused by a railroad telegrapher's key first closing and then rapidly being released.

Andrew's use of the telegraph on his DSP&P layout illustrates his solution to another consideration. When choosing a prototype to model, think of the action—work for crew members—or lack thereof. If you're a loner, one train at a time may be sufficient. But if you're part of a large operating group, as Andrew is, you'll need more activity to keep everyone busy when they show up at your house.

The Colorado narrow-gauge lines are hard to beat

Fig. 2-6: The Rio Grande's narrow-gauge lines in Colorado and New Mexico offer perpetual allure for modelers. The availability of working tourist lines like the Cumbres & Toltec Scenic and the Durango & Silverton turn a field trip for researching prototypes into a treat.

when it comes to mystique, scenery, and appealing hardware, but train frequency was relatively low. Trains were also comparatively short (fig. 2-6), which reduces yard work—not a good thing when "full employment" is the goal. Ensuring that each crew member is immersed in the situation—the why and how your railroad goes about its work—turns each job into a meaningful assignment. Andrew's use of telegraphed communications is but one example of how creativity can offset a lack of traffic density.

Trends

Prototype modelers have such a wealth of riches to choose from that it's hard to know which way to run first. I used to complain, for example, that I saw no reason for HO knuckle couplers and wheelsets to be oversized, because couplers half their

size and wheels half their width worked fine in N scale, thank you. HO modelers can now choose among several brands of near-scale couplers, and NorthWest Short Line and others offer replacement metal wheelsets that range from today's RP25 contour to semi-scale and even fine-scale dimensions. For years, I operated a small fleet of empty hopper cars equipped with NWSL's semi-scale ("code 88," or .088″ wide) wheels on track built to accommodate wheels of RP25 dimensions, and I can't recall a single derailment.

As new locomotives and cars are added to the roster, I'm buying or equipping them with "scale" magnetic couplers. Until the railroad is operational, I won't know whether there is a downside to this move, but tests of long trains have been encouraging. Potential for trouble exists if the couplers can move vertically in their boxes and slip out of the adjoining knuckle, but if N scale modelers can deal with even tighter tolerances, why should the same situation be an undue hassle in HO?

If couplers must be aligned more accurately to "make the joint" when coupling cars,

so be it. Couplers don't always line up when the pros try to couple cars, so it's not a truly automatic operation anyway. Since we don't even have to couple up the air hoses, there's no reason to complain about extra work.

Coupling cars occasionally will prove problematic. However, uncoupling them almost always is. Magnetic couplers—like those Kadee introduced to the hobby decades ago, bless them—feature dangling steel "air hoses" that a permanent or electro-magnet located between the rails will push to one side when slack is taken above the magnet.

However, permanent magnets don't look good, can cause unwanted uncouplings, can't be located every place cars need to be uncoupled, and require that couplers be maintained to a set of high standards. Electro-magnets can be hidden, but are more expensive and difficult to install. In addition, the knuckle operating wire, which does not look much like an air hose, interferes with a scale air-hose casting.

Modelers have devised many solutions to address this problem. Dan Holbrook mounts permanent magnets

in plastic trays hidden below the ties. The trays allow the magnets to be pushed sideways between the rails to uncouple a car. The magnets can also be pulled to one side to prevent inadvertent uncouplings. A choke cable and knob connects the crew member to the magnet.

Other hobbyists utilize skewers or bent wires, some mounted on small flashlights to aid their tired eyes as they try to stick the skewer inside the coupler knuckle or pull an "air hose" to one side. Accurail's Switchman plastic skewer works like a charm with that firm's magnetic couplers—less reliably with others. Skewers allow the metal wire to be cut off and a scale air hose added for a prototypical appearance, but techniques requiring the "air hose" to be pulled to one side won't work after the wire has been trimmed off.

Multi-deck railroads add to the problem. It will be at minimum hard or at worst impossible for a crewmember to position his or her head above the couplers to align the skewer. L-shaped "pull-wire" uncouplers work better in those situations if the air hoses haven't been trimmed off. How you plan to have

Fig. 2-7: Budget restrictions make one- or two-horse short lines like the Narragansett Pier (above) attractive modeling options. Don't forget the interchange with a trunk line, as at Bath, New York, between the Bath & Hammondsport and the Erie Lackawanna (left). Both of these prototype photos date to May 1972.

crews uncouple cars should be considered a part of the layout design process, since it may affect how you detail your cars.

Acquiring needed models

It may seem as though modelers of some railroads have all the luck. The models they need to represent their prototypes seem to roll out of the factories like boxes of Cheerios. If you're serious about modeling a specific prototype, you will need to make a careful inventory of what's available or has been announced. Anyone who

picks the Pennsy or Santa Fe is going to have an easier row to hoe than will those who fancy a small short line that operated with some weird industrial switcher.

Wise tradeoffs can be made. Modeling a railroad in a large area suggests a need for many locomotives, but you'll be likely to find them commercially available. If they're up to your standards or can easily be upgraded and you can afford them, you're off to a good start.

Conversely, you could model a branch of a larger railroad or a small railroad

or short line (fig. 2-7) that ran one or a few intriguingly eccentric locomotives, each of which represents a major kitbashing or scratchbuilding project. The reduced scope of that project—its smaller yard and engine terminal, fewer large industries, and so on— should mean you'll have more time to spend on the engine-building projects.

Or, to save time, you may opt for finding custom builders who specialize in assembling or detailing your locomotives to specifications. You may also find that you can make trades—you'll help

Sue wire or scenick her railroad if she'll detail or airbrush a bunch of locomotives or cars for you.

Perhaps the problem is as simple as having commercial models painted and lettered specifically for your railroad. Ordering a run of several hundred hoppers be custom-lettered for your railroad isn't much more expensive than buying a comparable number of factory-lettered kits. Prototype modelers have an advantage over freelancers because they may be able to interest a manufacturer in producing the needed model using a stock kit.

Working with the pros

I recommend that budding prototype modelers get to know professional railroaders who worked for their favorite railroad. Many of them can

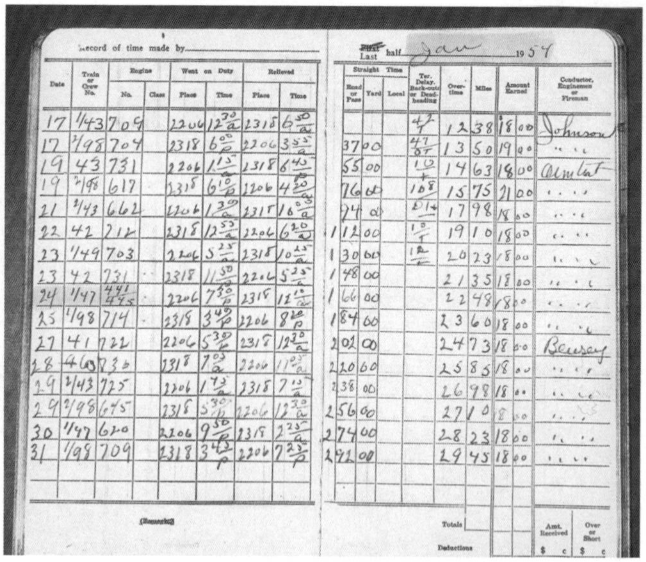

Fig. 2-8: When evaluating a prototype for inspiration, look at the control panels as well. The mini-CTC panel shown above once controlled the NKP-Monon crossing and NKP passing track's east switch at Linden, Indiana.

Fig. 2-9: Employee time books, which were used to record hours worked as a basis for getting paid, provide useful insights. The open pages at above right verify that in Frankfort, Indiana, in 1954, 700s (Berkshires) and 600s (Mikados) still ruled, although on January 24 a pair of 400s (GP7s) stuck a wheel in the door on First 47.

often be found at railroad-specific conventions. As modelers, we tend to think we know how a railroad operated and why, but odds are that the professionals did it differently. Union working agreements often affected the way a particular task was actually performed. Our job as prototype modelers is to understand how and why.

In my operations book, I cited an example of a routing for a boxcar headed from timber country to a lumberyard in central Indiana. I postulated that the car would be interchanged

by the Nickel Plate to the Pennsylvania and then would be delivered to the lumberyard's siding on the PRR. But a former Pennsy man who worked that job said it would be too expensive for them to move it a hundred feet or so from the NKP interchange to the customer's siding, so the NKP typically spotted such cars on their team track and let the customer get the lumber. Outstanding service? No. Efficiency? Perhaps. Reality? Ah, that's the point.

In Indiana, the NKP had some manual block territory. There, operators provided the same function as block signals by checking with another operator down the line to ensure the block between them was clear before allowing a train to enter it. Indiana upped the ante by passing a law stating that two trains could not meet—that is, they could not occupy the same block— in manual block territory without receiving authorization to do so on a Form 31 train order. Unlike more common Form 19 orders, Form 31 orders had to be physically signed by the conductor and engineer, which meant they had to stop their train.

On most Third Subdivision passing tracks in Indiana, the NKP got around this by locating one turnout next to the depot or tower and equipping the operator with an interlocked mini-Centralized Traffic Control panel that operated the entrance switch (fig. 2.8). By having the operator route one of the opposing trains into the siding within interlocking limits, both trains would not be in the same block at the same time, and the meet could be arranged on a Form 19.

As a prototype modeler, I will replicate this practice in spirit by having one end of each passing track controlled from a mini-CTC panel on the fascia near the depot. The more distant siding switch will be controlled by a lever or toggle that simulates the operation of a ground throw operated by a crew. If the operator assigned to that town, among others, happens to be in that town as a train approaches, I'll expect him or her to operate the CTC panel, but not the distant manual switch. This adds to the realism of both jobs— which is a major objective for the prototype modeler.

Don Daily, a retired Norfolk Southern engineer

who broke in as a fireman on NKP steam out of Frankfort, Indiana, has been a key source of information and inspiration for my Third Sub project. One of his most important contributions, beyond an excellent memory, has been to obtain copies of fellow railroaders' time books. Railroaders' pay was tied to the time they worked, and they dutifully recorded the date, train, tonnage, engines, points at either end of the run, conductor's or engineer's name, and, at times, even caboose number.

By checking Don's and several other employees' time books, I've been able to build an accurate picture of the steam locomotives still in service when the first GP7s (fig. 2-9) and RS-3s were used on that subdivision. I've also discerned the typical tonnage and the situations when trains doubled Cayuga Hill (as evidenced by higher-than-usual mileage figures between terminals).

But will it play in Peoria?

Balancing your modeling objectives with constraints of time, money, knowledge, skill, product availability, and other important factors is tough. Done haphazardly, plausibility suffers.

CHAPTER THREE
Plausibility

Plausibility is not the same as realism. A perfectly realistic model placed in an unlikely setting—a Union Pacific 4-8-8-4 on an eastern short line, to give one example—will pummel plausibility. Regardless of how grand a job is done on the modeling, a portrayal of something as unusual as a steam locomotive operating alongside a second-generation hood unit (fig. 3-1) will detract from your railroad's plausibility. In short, to create a plausible model railroad, you need to consider modeling not just the railroad hardware but the essentials that comprise day-to-day railroading.

Fig. 3-1: Just because it happened doesn't make it plausible. This photograph of the Allegheny Midland raises eyebrows, despite the prototype shot of the Reading & Northern in April 1991. Modeling the ordinary instead of the highly unusual is often the path to plausibility.

Drawing the line

Whether you're freelancing or modeling a specific prototype, plausibility results from the way everything works when considered as a whole. The quest for plausibility beyond realism encompasses stationary as well as operating models, the scenery that complements them, the way the models operate, their context, and the tasks assigned to crew members.

On his HO scale Cat Mountain & Santa Fe, David Barrow has achieved a high level of plausibility. Although quite a few of the freight cars lettered for the CMSF follow Santa Fe painting guidelines, he ensured that no one would fail to appreciate his theme of basing the railroad in Texas by using locomotives lettered only for parent ATSF (fig. 3-2).

It might be possible to model prototype railroading down to the last nuance, but that task could be onerous. Many details aren't readily visible, and some railroad jobs aren't much fun to do or take forever to complete. Sitting in the cab of an SD40-2 parked on a passing track for an hour or two waiting for an approaching train can lull an insomniac to sleep.

Jack Burgess pondered what it would take to model every last foot of his favorite prototype, the Yosemite Valley Railroad in central California. He concluded that much of the run would become repetitive and would be stretched out over a long period, and thus would become boring, just as it did for the professionals.

All things considered, Jack's much-condensed HO version of the Yosemite Valley RR that was built

Fig. 3-2: Unlike a setting that commands a second look, paint schemes of the cars and locomotives as well as the scenery on David Barrow's freelanced HO scale Cat Mountain & Santa Fe, seen above, fit his portrayal of the Santa Fe in Texas. To ensure plausibility, David didn't stray far from reality. Tommy Holt photo.

within the confines of his California garage represents an excellent compromise in the never-ending battle of aspiration versus practicality.

Fig. 3-3: Taken at the end of the Penn Central era in June 1976, this photo shows that the Pennsylvania Railroad's Port Road hugging the cliffs high above the Susquehanna River was indeed electrified—but in a post-1980 setting, this would not be plausible.

Does it add up?

Whether the objective is to freelance in a realistic manner or model a specific prototype, we face concerns about whether our decisions are plausible in their totality. You can, for example, scratchbuild or superdetail a gleaming brass model of a steam locomotive for your 1950s railroad. But are you willing to apply a grungy paint and weathering job to that crown jewel so it looks as though it has been in its last months of service? If not, plausibility will suffer.

Modeling enthusiasts approach the hobby from a variety of viewpoints. On one extreme is the hobbyist who wants every detail to be as realistic and plausible as possible. On the other extreme is the modeler who asks, "If we want to run steam locomotives next to U-boats, who's to say we can't?"

Plausibility says we can't. We must come to a personal reckoning where plausibility is concerned. If we model alone in our homes, we can set the rules. It's when we communicate our vision to others—by sharing our work—that plausibility moves to the front burner. Then, either we have to find compatriots who share our lack of concern about some obvious discrepancies, then convince them that such clangers are justified by other goals, and resolve to be more attentive to harmony of time and place in the future—or wind up ignoring everyone while whistling "My Way."

Just as individual railroads don't exist in a vacuum, our layouts take shape in a world filled with people who know a lot about railroads large and small. Those who will be seeing our railroads have expectations, and some of those preconceived notions have to do with our creation's plausibility. Building and operating a railroad plausible enough to reflect reality takes considerable skill.

Some modelers think that this sounds limiting, even intimidating, but it's actually a blessing. Few of us have the artistic skills to create a new world in miniature that will be truly convincing. For most modelers, it's easier to learn to carefully observe the real world in its current or past forms—and then edit key parts of it to a practical form—than it would be to reinvent the flanged wheel.

Measuring up

That the hobby has become more focused on prototype modeling is readily apparent. Where we once bemoaned the market's lack of a plastic model for an Alco RS-3, we now ask what phase the model is and whether both the Digital Command Control (DCC) decoder and sound speaker will fit within the confines of its prototypical-width hood.

Fig. 3-4: The South Shore mixed passenger service with a healthy freight business handled by ex-New York Central boxcabs and double-cab GE motors (above). Sisters on the Milwaukee Road were dubbed "Little Joes" for their intended customer: Stalin's Russia.

Fig. 3-5: Like finding a dinosaur in the jungle, seeing steeple-cab electrics (right) still eking out a living on Iowa Traction in Mason City in the 21st century is a treat.
To avoid runaround moves, two crewmembers park two or three motors strategically and change from one to another as required.

And where we once regarded the term "ready-to-run" as being a euphemism for "toy-like," we are now likely to gobble up relatively pricey RTR boxcars and built-up structures like popcorn.

The flip side of this drive toward greater realism is intimidation. I've heard even veteran modelers complain that today's push toward super-critical prototype modeling is bringing about the ruination of the hobby. Who, they ask, can measure up to such high standards?

Other modelers find it hard to stake their claim to virgin territory. A friend asked me whether any of the NKP Clover Leaf District's four subdivisions had yet to be "spoken for" by another modeler. He wanted to do something new and different, not follow the crowd. It's fun being a pioneer.

The concern is that unless we're willing to spend forever and a day researching a given prototype and then building models that are suitable for museum display, our models and our railroads will not measure up. We'll be shamed out of the club: "Turn in your throttle, sir. Your kind isn't welcome here anymore!"

Whether we are inspired or intimidated is largely a matter of our attitude and choice of goals. If I were to focus not on doing a credible job of modeling the NKP in 1954 but on measuring up to the standards of all my friends taken collectively, I'd probably take up some easier hobby—say, building, then trying to fly and, shudder, land a quarter-scale, radio-controlled model of a four-engine B-17G bomber in a stiff crosswind.

Some of my friends are experts in freight car and locomotive construction and detailing or in the arcane art of operation by timetable and train orders. Others I know, especially those who worked for the Nickel Plate, are more knowledgeable about my favorite prototype than I'll ever be. Still others take care to shape and detail their railroads' physical plants from

rail braces on turnouts to drainage ditch profiles with incredible precision. On the face of it, Allen McClelland's "good enough" philosophy doesn't seem to apply to these folks.

My task is not to go nuts trying to keep up with the Casey Joneses but rather to identify facets of railroading and my chosen prototype that are meaningful to me. As long as the results are consistent and plausible as a whole, the railroad will meet my objectives and not offend knowledgeable observers.

However, if something will be hard to change, I try to get it right the first time. Because it would be difficult to increase my minimum radius by a foot if the curve makes my steam locomotives and full-length passenger cars look implausible, I do my homework first.

The impact of sound

If you contemplate almost anyone's modeling efforts, you'll find that people excel in some areas but work to more modest standards in others. Moreover, modelers will have some standards or major objectives that are at odds with your own. Another model railroad designer's pet passion may not even be on your radar screen.

I consider diesel and steam sound systems a requirement for a railroad. They provide the realism I expect. No sound, no railroad. To me, it's as simple as that. I no longer find it plausible to hear a locomotive quietly humming along the rails when I know that it should be making a lot of specific noises. (In many instances, it should also be producing a lot of black smoke, but I prefer that my models do this as seldom as possible.)

My opinion can be an expensive one to put into practice. It also creates some technical hassles. For those and other reasons, I doubt that many of my regular operators agree with me on the subject. No matter. Here's an example of the way my requirement plays out.

A major factor motivating me to convert to digital command control was my wish to gain access to diesel sound. I also wanted the capability of using headlights and whistle and horn signals during operating sessions.

Test runs with a trio of sound-equipped Proto 2000 NKP GP7s confirmed my views about sound. As I barely cracked open the throttle, the sound system suggested the 567-series prime movers were now in run 2 or 3 (of a total of 8 notches on standard EMD and Alco throttles), yet there was little perceptible motion. Clearly, those Geeps were struggling to start a heavy train. A bit more throttle and they jumped up to run 4 or 5 and began to accelerate the train. When I opened the throttle even wider, they revved up to run 8 and broke into that distinctive EMD "song." Then, to my delight, they momentarily dropped to idle (without slowing down) to simulate a transition—motor circuits switching from series to series-parallel and finally to parallel—then came back to full power.

I was ecstatic! A trio of "plain-vanilla" Geeps, which is about as basic as motive power gets, knocked my socks off. I spent the next hour just running the train back and forth, something I haven't done since I got a Lionel O-27 set for Christmas well

Fig. 3-6: With the demise of the ex-Virginian and the Milwaukee's electrified lines, freight electrification in the United States retreated to the ex-PRR and New Haven lines, plus a few isolated utility-owned coal haulers, such as the Muskingum Electric in southeastern Ohio.

over half a century ago. Model railroading has entered a new era: the Sound Age.

The train took far more time to get moving with sound on than off because I wanted to hear and enjoy each change of prime-mover rpm. These distinctions are of critical importance on a model railroad, as distances are short and everything we do, no matter how simple, has to have some "play value" while contributing to realism.

Plausibility parameters

The good news for those of us whose knowledge of the hobby and ambitions have limits is that plausibility is not about counting rivets. It has more to do with achieving a consistent and reasonable level within our modeling endeavors. If everything we are attempting

Fig. 3-7: Use of smaller-scale structures in the background to suggest greater distance can be effective if the viewing angle can be controlled. The distant barn and farmhouse in this convincing scene on photographer Paul Dolkos' HO Boston & Maine layout are actually in N scale.

to do fits into a greater scheme of things that makes sense to the average viewer, we create a plausible railroad.

Specific things will bother some among us more than others. An example can be found in *Model Railroad Planning 2004*. The Norfolk & Western transition-era modeler Rich Weyand explained why his good friend Bill Pistello, who works in the signaling department of a full-sized railroad, put such emphasis on building an extremely accurate signaling system for his own N scale railroad:

"It is not possible to model a significant portion of a major railroad in a completely prototypical way within a reasonable amount of space or time. . . . Compromising something you're intimately familiar with will be more bothersome than it will be to cut corners elsewhere."

Rich's point is that any errors in signaling application or function would instantly be apparent to Bill and diminish the quality of his modeling experience. If he

has to make compromises, it's better that he do so in areas that don't reflect adversely on his professional skills and knowledge.

It pays for each of us to be aware of areas where undue compromise will adversely affect our enjoyment of the hobby and work hard to avoid them. But we can't hold every part of the process to such lofty standards and still get our railroads built and operating, so we have to be prepared to accept compromises that will allow us to forge ahead.

Changing times

Let's consider a type of full-sized railroading—the electrified railroad—as an example of applying the parameters of plausibility. Portions of several major railroads in the United States were at one time electrified, much as the Northeast Corridor between Boston and Washington, D.C. is today. In that category fell the Milwaukee Road's two western electrified sections, the Great Northern's line through the Cascades, the

Virginian's wires spanning a challenging area of the rugged Appalachians, the Pennsylvania's long stretches of catenary (fig. 3-3), the Boston & Maine's electrified line through Hoosac Tunnel, the New Haven along the north shore of Long Island Sound, the New York Central's lines north of New York City, and even the Cleveland Union Terminal's electrification, among others.

Electric locomotives may lack some of the aural dynamics of a hard-working diesel-electric or steam locomotive; nonetheless, a unique form of visual magic occurs on railroading that takes place under overhead wires.

I got an early dose of low-key electrified railroading when I lived a few miles south of the Mason City & Clear Lake electric freight line in north-central Iowa in the 1940s. Incredibly, the railroad is still operating under wire as Iowa Traction, serving seasonally busy grain elevators southwest of downtown Mason City by using traction-orange motors of various ancestry (fig. 3.5).

A move to west-central Indiana in 1951 engendered my fascination with the Nickel Plate, but we wound up in Michigan City, where the Chicago South Shore & South Bend used several types of electric locomotives, including the massive 800s to move freights on this busy commuter line (fig. 3-4). Imagine driving your car on 11th Street and coming face-to-face with one of those behemoths! The South Shore relied more on catenary and pantographs than on trolley poles. For model railroads, that fact is a boon, because no pole changing is required for backup moves.

Railfanning jaunts took me to the New Haven and Pennsylvania electrified lines, but I missed seeing the Virginian and Milwaukee Road under catenary. I was nonetheless sufficiently impressed with big-time electric railroading to make plans to electrify the climb from Sunrise, Virginia, up to the West Virginia state line on the Allegheny Midland. To do so, I acquired a three-motor set of Virginian jack-

Fig. 3-8: Jim Boyd's foggy-morning photograph of Quinnimont, West Virginia (top), inspired the author to use Chesapeake & Ohio structures as prototypes for Allegheny Midland lineside buildings. The model of well-known QN Cabin was scratchbuilt and became "BJ Cabin" on the AM (bottom).

Fig. 3-9: The author initially combined graphic elements of the as-delivered and post-1959 NKP paint schemes to create the unique yet similar scheme seen on the RSD-12 (above, at right). The result proved distracting and raised too many questions. So he painted other AM units to match actual NKP schemes or substituted AM lettering for the NKP's on factory-painted NKP units.

shaft "square heads" and planned to leave one in VGN livery rusting in the weeds—a parts source for the other two motors refurbished for use as pushers on the AM.

Unfortunately for this plan's fruition, the railroad's gradual modernization over the next few years made an electrified model less and less plausible (fig. 3-6). Those of you who model an earlier time may find that electrified railroading offers fascinating opportunities.

Forced perspective

In model railroading, the term "forced perspective" often refers to using smaller-scale structures in the background to suggest greater distances. Done carefully, it can be an effective way to fool viewers into seeing more depth than is actually there (fig. 3-7). When composing a photograph, this technique can be reversed to good effect by judiciously placing larger-scale models in the foreground. Their size leads viewers to believe that the smaller background objects are farther away than they actually are.

An imperfect example

My Allegheny Midland offered a workable example of plausible freelancing. The name identified its locale. Its nickname, the Midland Road, tied it to its parent, the Nickel Plate Road. This theme was underscored by using custom decals that mimic the NKP's distinctive lettering style. I also used

NKP prototypes for most rolling stock, although some Chesapeake & Ohio steam locomotives were used (fig. 6-13). This was not a big stretch, as the NKP and C&O were at one time jointly owned by the Van Sweringen brothers.

Early in the planning process, I became a big fan of C&O depot architecture. I recall the evening when Jim Boyd showed me a slide of the combination yardmaster's office–interlocking tower at Quinnimont, West Virginia —QN Cabin, in C&O parlance (fig. 3-8). I decided on the spot that AM's lineside structures would follow C&O prototypes.

At the time, it all seemed to fit together seamlessly, but in retrospect there were a few discordant notes. Take Quinnimont's yard office. Wasn't it confusing to see that well-known structure labeled "BJ" instead of "QN"? Do such mixed messages

hurt plausibility?

Therein lies a dilemma for the prototype-based free-lancer. If opting to model standard, ordinary structures from a specific prototype, it's easy to give a freelanced rail-road a cloak of plausibility. But modelers tend to favor the exceptional rather than the mundane. That can create confusing visual clues about the location and ownership of the railroad.

The Allegheny Midland's Nickel Plate rolling stock was easily justified. The NKP controlled the AM, so there was no reason for Midland Road to not embrace typical NKP steam locomotive designs, diesel types, and standards for painting and lettering equipment.

In fact, I came to regret the only time I ventured even a short distance from NKP diesel paint standards. The first two units I painted for the AM were a pair of Alco RSD-12s, slightly longer, six-traction-motor versions of the better-known RS-11. Instead of copying the NKP paint scheme (fig. 3-9), I put my own "brand" on it with slight modifications. It was a plausible combination of the NKP's as-delivered and post-1959 simplified schemes, but it never rang true to me. Subsequent units followed NKP paint specifications.

CHAPTER FOUR
Considerations of time

Fig. 4-1: Regional railroads that take over parts of trunk lines often make do with used locomotives and a minimum of new paint. Here an ex-Green Bay & Western Alco joins forces with a chop-nosed Geep sporting abbreviated NKP-like stripes on the Kankakee, Beaverville & Southern's former NKP line west of Lafayette, Indiana, in June 1999. John Roberts photographed this former Mexican RS-11 of equal esthetic attributes on his O scale Blue Ridge & Southern.

When we think of time as it affects a model railroad, we usually think in terms of which era we choose to model or perhaps the ticking of the fast-time clock that regulates the pace of our operating sessions. Choosing the era, year, or even month that's the most "feature rich" can be a daunting yet rewarding task. However, other aspects of time selection and depiction, among them "extrapolating" and conveying the passage of time, are worth consideration.

Choosing a late-steam era for the Allegheny Midland

Event	1953	1954	1955	1956	1957	1958	1959
Ex-W&LE J-1 4-8-2s still in service	Yes	No	No	No	No	No	No
Ex-W&LE I-3 2-6-6-2s still in service	Yes	Yes	Yes	No	No	No	No
Ex-W&LE S-4 2-8-4s still on W&LE	Yes	Yes	Yes	Yes	Yes	No	No
NKP G-9 2-8-0s on Wheeling Dist.	No	No	No	Yes?	Yes	No	No
NKP S, S-1 Berkshires on Wheeling Dist.	No	No	No	No	Yes	No	No
Alco RSD-12s in service on NKP	No	No	No	No	Yes	Yes	Yes
EMD SD9s in service on NKP	No	No	No	No	Yes	Yes	Yes
New diesel paint scheme adopted	No	No	No	No	No	No	Yes

Fig. 4-2: A pair of GE Dash 9s, one in the classic Santa Fe red warbonnet and the other in BNSF livery, moves tonnage west of Chicago on Bruce Carpenter's HO layout. Within reasonable limits, this consist alone is sufficient to establish the era he depicts. Bruce Carpenter photo.

Fig. 4-3: As the chart at left shows, the goal to operate NKP S and S-1 Berkshires along with newly delivered RSD-12s and SD9s made 1957 the best choice for the Allegheny Midland's transition back into the steam era.

Somewhere in time

If you like what you see down at trackside today, you're set in terms of selecting an era to model. Models of most of the latest products from General Electric and Electro-Motive are available, and many older units are still cranking out the ton-miles for their original or subsequent owners. Regional and shortline railroads often purchase used locomotives (fig. 4-1), so a model of a 21st-century railroad may be able to employ locomotives built in the 1970s or earlier.

If an earlier era has appeal, now is the time to refine its parameters. You may want to make or expand a chart, such as the one shown in fig. 4-3, which I made to help me focus on an optimum year as the Allegheny Midland shifted back to the steam-diesel transition era.

If you model 1968, for example, you can use equipment lettered for the

Fig. 4-4: Weathering structures suggests that a model railroad is part of a time continuum. The author simulated smoke and soot on the AM's coal dock at Sunrise, Virginia (above left), by using washes of Polly Scale black and grimy black. A building along the Chesapeake & Ohio in West Virginia (above right) makes an ideal reference when simulating peeling paint and roof texturing. Note the brighter green roof patches indicating repairs to the structure in the background.

Penn Central (as well as predecessor roads) but not the Chessie System, which debuted in 1973, or Amtrak, which started in 1971. If you plan to model the Spokane, Portland & Seattle, Great Northern, Northern Pacific, or Burlington, you'll want to pick an era before 1970, when they merged to form the Burlington Northern, which, in 1995, merged with the Santa Fe to form the BNSF (fig. 4-2). Modeling the Milwaukee's electrified era sets the clock prior to 1974—unless you opt to

revise history and upgrade the line with new hood-style electrics from GE, an intriguing premise for a freelanced Milwaukee Road.

The desire to run a specific type of equipment may pick an era for you, as exemplified by the Virginian's GE-built EL-C electric locomotives, available from Bachmann in HO scale. If you model the VGN and use EL-Cs, you set your timeframe as somewhere between their August 1955 delivery date and the N&W merger on December 1, 1959. The window is open wider than that, however, as the N&W left all but one of the EL-Cs in VGN paint (but did renumber them) until overhead power was shut off on June 30, 1962.

The cash-strapped New Haven got the EL-Cs for a pittance and put 11 of them into service as EF-4s between October 1963 through June 1965. They served the NYNH&H well until it disappeared into the Penn Central on January 1, 1969. PC and then (as of April 1, 1976) Conrail used ten of them as E33s, mainly

between Enola (near Harrisburg), Pennsylvania, and Potomac Yard near Washington, D.C., until March 31, 1981. With due allowance for overlapping paint schemes following mergers, these dates establish time "bookends" for prototype modelers.

Jim Kelly prepared a chart for the July 1987 *Model Railroader* showing when various types of diesels were produced. It's still useful for those modeling the mid-1980s or before. By refining the chart to show when specific units were delivered to your favorite railroad(s), it helps you focus on an appropriate period.

Railroad Model Craftsman also published useful "Raildates" charts, compiled by Charles Buccola, that showed milestones by year. The January 1979 issue, for example, listed key dates for locomotives ("1946: Alco RS-2, FA-1, and PA-1 introduced"), cars ("1967: Thrall-Door boxcar introduced"), trackwork ("1927: CTC first placed in operation on NYC"), and general history ("1957:

L&N/NC&StL merger; abandonment of the NYO&W").

It takes a little homework to uncover key dates and define an era, but you may find that the research is as interesting and rewarding as the modeling. A good place to start is *Trains* Magazine's monthly timeline of major events, from 10, 25, and 50 years ago.

Picking a year

My neighbor Perry Squier models the Pittsburg, Shawmut & Northern in 1923. Why 1923 and not 1925 or even 1940? The Shawmut scrapped a sizable portion of its roster in 1924, and Perry didn't want to lose the opportunity to model the earlier 4-4-0s and several other locomotives.

Of course, Perry could have broadened the definition of his modeled era to "the 1920s," but he felt that narrowing his focus would be more rewarding. It can be challenging to uncover what happened on a small Pennsylvania coal hauler in a specific year so many decades ago, but Perry

Fig. 4-5: Track coloration shows usage and passage of time, as indicated by the busy Erie Lackawanna main line near Narrowsburg, New York, in June 1974 (top) and a less-used secondary line (bottom). Sand on ascending grades can lighten rail; brake-shoe residue on down-grades imparts a rusty hue.

found the benefits commensurate with the effort expended. He even developed new friendships along the way with others who admire the PS&N.

Extrapolating history

As mentioned in chapter one, extrapolation is one good approach to freelancing. The Virginian merged into the Norfolk & Western in 1959, for example. You could assume that the N&W kept its hands off the VGN, which put the classic black-and-yellow paint scheme applied to Fairbanks-Morse Train Masters on a brace of Alco Century 628s, EMD SD40-2s, or GE U36Cs.

But we should use care when revising history in what appears to be our favor. I have always enjoyed seeing an A-B-B-A set of F3s or F7s up front on freight trains, so I pondered whether my NKP-controlled Midland Road might have been persuaded by a resourceful diesel drummer from EMD to buy F7s. After all, EMD did paint a pair of F7 demonstrators in an NKP-inspired livery (fig. 5-3).

However, retired EMD design engineer Bill Darnaby reminded me to keep in mind the scope of the railroad. Since the AM was a relatively small railroad, it wouldn't have taken long to completely dieselize. Had the AM bought F7s in 1948, then in all likelihood it would have been fully

dieselized long before 1957.

What's so special about 1957? That's the year the NKP took delivery of Alco RSD-12s and EMD SD9s, which I wanted to model (fig. 4-2). I also wanted to feature AM steam on the roster. Moreover, in 1957 some old friends from Indiana—class S and S-1 Berkshires displaced from the St. Louis and Sandusky Divisions by Geeps and RS-3s—saw service on the

NKP's Wheeling District, which connected end-to-end with the Allegheny Midland. So 1957 it was.

A review of dieselization dates confirmed the sagacity of Bill's advice. In June 1953, the Southern, a major buyer of F units, was the first major railroad to completely dieselize. The Clinchfield, a railroad of similar size and scope to the AM, dieselized early with Fs, and its steam fleet—even the modern

UP-style Challengers—was cold long before 1957. The Western Maryland also bought Fs to retire steam by the early '50s, as did the Reading. Even a much larger coal hauler such as the Chesapeake & Ohio, which initially dieselized with F units, barely made it to the mid-decade point before dropping steam's fires when it could finally get all the diesels it wanted.

Conversely, consider the

Fig. 4-6: Even brand-new GEs working their way west from Erie, Pennsylvania, in September 1993 show little evidence of shine. The Western Maryland F unit being washed at Hagerstown, Maryland, in May 1971 will not look as shiny after the water has dried.

eastern railroads that ran steam into the late 1950s. The Norfolk & Western held off EMD and Alco until late in the game, then dieselized not with Fs and FAs but with Geeps and RSs. The same thing occurred on the Illinois Central and the Nickel Plate. The era of the F unit was gone by then, as the utility of the hood unit had become clear.

Much as I enjoy watching Fs at work, that image was wrong for the Midland Road. Parent NKP didn't do it that way, and it was implausible for a relatively small railroad set in 1957 to boast both Fs and steam.

Whether to weather

Weathering used to be a highly controversial topic. Back when brass locomotives were regarded more as crown jewels for display than as fodder for detailing, weathering, and operation, one seldom saw such priceless artifacts looking as grungy as their prototypes.

A reluctance to weather models was perhaps even more common in the formative years of our hobby, when most cars and locomotives had to be painstakingly built from scratch or difficult kits. Why spend all that time perfecting a model, it was argued, and then make the thing look like it had sat out in the backyard all winter? That the shiny models were highly implausible didn't seem to bother anyone.

How far we've come! Like silky-smooth mechanisms and fidelity to prototype, weathering that suggests the age and usage of a model is almost commonplace. Now it's the lack of weathering that catches a viewer's eye.

One of the best examples of "aging" that I have seen was an HO model of an

EMD SW1500 built by Wayne Sittner. It was obviously a former Reading unit, as its tattered and faded green-and-yellow livery proclaimed, but the RDG diamond herald had been painted black with stenciled "CR" letters, as if hastily applied shortly after the 1976 formation of Conrail.

As a railfan, such desecration of a once-proud paint scheme would have irked me to my bone marrow. But Wayne's model looked exactly right. It had to be prototypical—no modeler in his or her right mind could have concocted that paint scheme.

There's no way to create such a signature model that marks a turning point in rail history without "weathering." To a greater or lesser degree,

Fig. 4-7: To ease a boxcar shortage during the 1970s, many obscure short lines wound up represented by new or freshly shopped boxcars that roamed the nation's rails collecting per diem fees. Railbox cars also filled this void. After the crisis ebbed and the cars were sent "home," the sponsoring railroads were hard pressed to find places to store them.

each model should show its age, usage, and heritage in a similar manner. Not every car and locomotive can possibly be fresh out of the builder's erecting halls or railroad's paint shop. Only a handful of very short lines (fig. 2-6) can lavish the TLC on a one-horse roster needed to give it the spit-and-polish look of a corporate business jet.

Fig. 4-8: Glimpses of what was here yesterday can be represented by foundations in the weeds—like those from a water tank at Lime Springs, Virginia (left)—or by evidence of a one-time interior wall on a store in Ohio City, Ohio, in September 2003 (above).

We often debate the color of concrete—gray or tan? But during the steam era, a concrete coal dock was soot black. Even a heavy weathering job is inadequate (fig. 4-4). For the many structures whose original coat of paint is past its prime, it's often better to paint a structure gray and then dry-brush on a color coat.

Planning ahead

Too often, aging a model is an afterthought. We paint models as though they were built yesterday, then try to dress them in an overcoat of time. It's usually easier to start the aging process at the same time you begin to build or assemble a model. It's not hard to distress the wood on a trestle's pilings or to slip a knife blade under a few

clapboards on an older house or depot, pry them loose at one end, and glue them down slightly askew—unless the model is already finished. If you're not sure how to proceed, just consult the instructions included with many high-end craftsman structure kits.

Be careful not to overdo such effects, however. I've seen supposedly lived-in houses and working factories that local building authorities would have condemned long before. Some aspects of "texturing" have to be exaggerated to show up in the smaller scales, but there's a clear distinction between realism and caricature.

And don't forget the track. Nothing kills realism faster than shiny rails. Coloration is affected by usage, as shown

by the two photos in fig. 4-5. A coat of Roof Brown is a good place to start, using Rail Brown and Rust for detailing as usage suggests. I prefer to start with weathered rail, as it provides a tooth for additional weathering applications to adhere to.

That plastic shine

Having more than a handful of spanking-new locomotives or cars quickly spoils any sense of realism an otherwise ably designed and well-built model railroad may aspire to. Since we typically view full-sized equipment and structures through several or even hundreds of yards of atmosphere, we seldom see a factory-fresh finish (fig. 4-6). Even units fresh out of the wash rack soon dry to a clean, but semi-flat, finish, and roofs seldom get really clean.

Although most model manufacturers are applying excellent finishes to their products, it's not hard to tone down the plastic sheen on

older models. A light spray of Testor's Dullcote from a can or airbrush is usually a good start. It's then easy to wet the model and flow on some water-based colors to simulate streaks of dirt and exhaust and mud; if you don't like what you see, rinse it off and start over.

During the 1970s, a boxcar shortage led to car-service rules being changed to allow a high daily rental fee, called "incentive per diem," to be charged. Suddenly short lines that no one had ever heard of seemed to have huge fleets of boxcars running freely on the continent's rails (fig. 4-7).

The cars were actually owned by investors; when the shortage eased, there were huge surpluses of such cars. Many were sold to other operators and relettered, often by crudely painting over the old herald and reporting marks.

Railbox cars ("Next load, any road") were also part of the picture, and later some of them were acquired by railroads and given new reporting marks. Commercial models of such cars have been offered. Railroads such as the Rock Island that couldn't survive caused fleets of used freight cars to come on the market, so you could see a "Rock" boxcar sporting another railroad's reporting marks (see cover photo).

Fading factory paint

Fig. 4-9: These before-and-after photos show how Mike Rose used Testor's Dullcote plus alcohol oversprays to lighten the factory-applied color on a model. The resulting piece appears to have faded paint and/or a coating of dust. To this point, the effect was reversible by respraying the model with Dullcote. Thinned oil paint was then applied to simulate rust and lubricant streaks. Mike also took the photos.

Mike Rose discovered a highly useful paint-fading technique quite by accident. He was using a plant mister to spray 70 percent isopropyl alcohol onto a stretch of ballast as a wetting agent before applying diluted glue. The spray happened to splatter on a line of Conrail hoppers that he had recently painted, decaled, and sprayed with Testor's Dullcote. To his horror, he later discovered that the alcohol droplets had created lighter splotches everywhere they landed on the sides of those just-painted hoppers.

In desperation, he grabbed a can of Dullcote and resprayed the hoppers. Presto! The splotches disappeared, and they stayed gone once the Dullcote had dried. Rather than thanking his lucky stars and leaving it at that, as I probably would have done, Mike began thinking how this effect could be used to his advantage. Maybe it could lighten—that is, fade—the color of factory-painted models, such as the magenta

used on some Detroit, Toledo & Ironton cars that fades so quickly.

Mike experimented on a brand-new Walthers 86-foot auto-parts boxcar to see if he could replicate his experience with the hoppers. He sprayed the model with Dullcote, waited for it to dry, and then sprayed the alcohol. Result: "faded" paint!

To illustrate his technique for this book, Mike chose a Walthers Golden West auto-parts boxcar (fig. 4-9) because many of the prototype GVSR cars he has seen are heavily faded from exposure to the sun, rain, and other elements. All he did to the model before using the fading technique was apply paint to the truck sideframes and wheel faces—a mixture of Polly Scale Rust and Rail Brown. He then applied several coats of Dullcote to ensure full coverage.

Once the Dullcote had dried (no odor), Mike sprayed on a coat of isopropyl alcohol. "Be sure to use the 70 percent type," he cautions, "which is the most common

variety you'll find at a drugstore. The 90 percent type is what many modelers use to strip paint!"

Mike sprayed one horizontal surface at a time and let the alcohol evaporate. "No need to puddle it on," he advises. Other effects can be achieved by letting the alcohol run down a vertical surface. "Feel free to experiment," Mike urges, "as the process is completely reversible!"

As the alcohol dries, the fade starts to "bloom." In a few areas where the fade wasn't as deep as he wanted, Mike applied more alcohol with a brush.

The resulting model was well faded but a bit too bland for Mike's tastes. So he used artist's oil paints—raw and burnt umber, raw and burnt sienna, and black—right from the tube. He put a hint of color on the tip of the bristles and drybrushed the details to highlight them. By brushing the weld seams on the car sides, he was able to apply just enough color for them to stand out distinctly against the

faded and weathered background.

In addition, Mike "dirtied up" the area along the sills, added fresh rust to the trucks and springs, and applied a bit of straight black to the hinge points on the plug doors. He used the somewhat wiped-off brush with the black still on it to dirty up the door tracks. Mike also added the rust streaks often seen at the end of the door tracks from the roof down. As a final touch, he applied some rust to the roof to tone down the silver panels.

The resulting model has no more detail than the factory-fresh version, but it exudes plausibility and realism. It looks like it has been working for a living, not posing for a studio portrait. And it represents an ideal first step into weathering for neophyte modelers, as prior to the application of the oil paints, another coating of Dullcote is enough to restore the model to its original appearance. A very clever, and most useful, technique indeed!

Mike Rose, a pioneering freight car modeler, found a way to simulate faded paint on factory-painted models. Incredibly, the process is entirely reversible, so you can go back to the like-new appearance if you don't care

for your initial weathering efforts. (See sidebar: "Fading factory paint.")

What time is it?

Important as it is to make considered choices about the era your railroad will depict,

it's even more important that your models seem to be part of the time continuum. They were not all built yesterday, so they should show evidence of the passage of time.

Even structures that are no longer present and are

therefore represented only by their foundations or a scar on an adjoining store's wall (fig. 4-8) will help convince careful observers that your railroad and the communities it serves have a long and multi-faceted history.

CHAPTER FIVE

Image and graphics

Railroad graphic design didn't come into its own until the advent of lots of blank sheet metal on diesel locomotive carbodies. Previously, graphic imagery was focused primarily on a corporate logo (typically called a "herald" or "medallion"), public timetables and brochures, the occasional streamlined steam locomotive, and the interior of each line's premier passenger trains. With a few notable exceptions, Pullman green and Tuscan red were among the few colors in use until streamlined diesel cab units debuted.

Fig. 5-1A: Santa Fe F units and passenger-equipped U-boats pause at Chicago; they're wearing the red warbonnet scheme, which railfans generally regard as the premier passenger paint scheme ever applied to a diesel. But was it unique to the Santa Fe, as is often assumed? See the four images of fig. 5-1B on the following page.

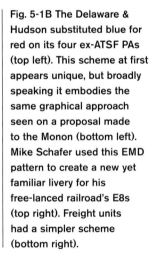

Fig. 5-1B The Delaware & Hudson substituted blue for red on its four ex-ATSF PAs (top left). This scheme at first appears unique, but broadly speaking it embodies the same graphical approach seen on a proposal made to the Monon (bottom left). Mike Schafer used this EMD pattern to create a new yet familiar livery for his free-lanced railroad's E8s (top right). Freight units had a simpler scheme (bottom right).

Early diesel paint schemes

If I say, "Santa Fe," what pops into your mind? My guess is red-nosed silver E and F units in their best-in-class warbonnet scheme (fig. 5-1A, page 35). Can you think of an example of a similar EMD passenger-unit paint scheme, or is this scheme unique to the ATSF?

Look at the four photos that make up fig. 5-1B. Notice that swash of red on a proposal that EMD made to the Monon; it used this general theme again in maroon on Rock Island units. You don't need a lot of imagination to see how a designer could derive any of these schemes from the other; it's mostly a matter of continuing the color down toward the fuel tank (Monon proposal) or gracefully rounding it off, then letting the stainless area project toward the nose (as in the ATSF scheme).

Now imagine how different either paint scheme would look in blue instead of red—which is the dominant color the Delaware & Hudson chose when they bought four ex-Santa Fe PAs. The overall effect is quite unlike the ATSF, even though they retained the basic graphic design. The Santa Fe used altered versions of this paint scheme, too, when they applied yellow warbonnets (with blue carbodies) to some freight units.

Mike Schafer's superb example of applying standard EMD design elements to a freelanced Illinois & St. Louis E8 demonstrates why it's important for a freelancer to understand how early paint schemes came to be. As Jim Boyd documented in the November 1984 and January 1985 issues of *Railfan & Railroad* and Andy Sperandeo illustrated in the November 1996 *Model Railroader*, most EMD E and F units, Geeps, and switchers wore paint schemes designed by only a handful of men and one woman there.

An as-delivered scheme for a freelanced railroad using EMD units should therefore exhibit some of those telltale graphic hallmarks.

The same constraints apply to most railroads that eschewed EMD in favor of early Baldwin (fig. 5-2) and Alco units. Each often exhibits company-specific graphic design elements that suggest which diesel maker created the paint scheme. The two photos shown in fig. 5-3 show what I mean.

In creating a paint scheme for a freelanced model railroad, having only modest graphic design skills or training may be an asset because one won't be tempted to be overly creative and thus miss capturing the prototype look. More good news: following a builder's example isn't difficult. It's easier to "crib" a scheme from a builder's standard graphics palette than to design a new one. You may even be able to reuse the carbody striping from a commercial decal set

Fig. 5-2: A typical Baldwin paint scheme incorporated a stripe with half-circle ends, as used here by the Durham & Southern. Electro-Motive typically used a less-rounded design, although there were exceptions (striping on Clinchfield F units, for example).

Fig. 5-3: The NKP's blue-and-aluminum-gray passenger scheme is an Alco design; EMD would have filled in the gray side panels with more than a stepped-down road name. EMD painted a pair of F7 demonstrators in a similar scheme with obvious EMD design cues. (Alco builder's photo from Bob's Photo; F7 photo courtesy John B. Corns.)

or mask a factory-painted unit to disguise its heritage by changing a body color.

Here's an easy test: if your freelanced first-generation diesel paint scheme doesn't seem at least vaguely familiar, you've probably gotten too creative. Mike Schafer's E8 (above) passed the test. Its blue and orange design is reminiscent of both the Rock Island and the Chicago & Eastern Illinois, both close neighbors of his I&StL.

You may recall that the

first paint applied to Allen McClelland's Virginian & Ohio freight units was an all-blue scheme (fig. 5-4). This represented the V&O of the late 1950s, when the country was in a recession. At that time, many railroads were simplifying their as-delivered schemes, including the Baltimore & Ohio (fig. 5-5), and the Clinchfield (fig. 1-5).

I've always wondered what the V&O's as-delivered scheme looked like, so I

asked Allen to create it for this book using standard EMD design elements (see drawings, p. 39). The blue-and-gray combination is an homage to the V&O's location near the Mason-Dixon line—blue for the Union and gray for the Confederacy. The pattern of the wide gray stripe is based on standard EMD design practices. For V&O passenger units, such as the EMD E6 and Alco PA-1, Allen added a touch

Fig. 5-4: When Allen
McClelland started to build
the HO scale Virginian & Ohio
in 1958, he modeled what he
saw: a trend toward more
simplified paint schemes.
V&O Fs got a "dip-blue"
scheme, while passenger
units got a modest nose
stripe. The top drawing
shows Allen's recent effort
to draw the as-delivered
schemes. Note how a change
of color and some striping—
either the EMD spear or a
Wabash-like V-stripe—create
an entirely new livery.

of class by using a black roof
and white stripes to match
the passenger car scheme.

Those modelers who want
to follow Allen's example
could change the scheme
substantially by selecting
different colors and adding
a thin stripe below the side
grills, perhaps ending in the
classic EMD "spear tip"
(fig. 5-6B). The wide stripe
could also be broken up into

a series of three parallel
stripes, along the lines of
paint schemes used on the
Boston & Maine (fig. 5-7)
and the Maine Central.

The photos in fig. 5-8
show how the Wabash
simplified its gray-and-blue
scheme by using a yellow
stripe to recall the former
gray-blue division line.
Bill Darnaby borrowed
from several EMD schemes,

Fig. 5-5: The Baltimore &
Ohio (above) was one of
many railroads that simplified
its diesel paint schemes in
the 1960s. The new scheme
saved money but didn't look
good. (Jim Boyd photo)

including the Southern
and the Wabash, to create
a scheme for his Maumee
passenger units that looks
like it's right out of EMD's

Fig. 5-6A: The top drawing shows Allen McClelland's recent drawing of the as-delivered V&O paint scheme. Note how a change of color and some striping—either the EMD "spear" or a Wabash-like V-stripe—create an essentially new livery, a typical EMD approach to diesel paint schemes.

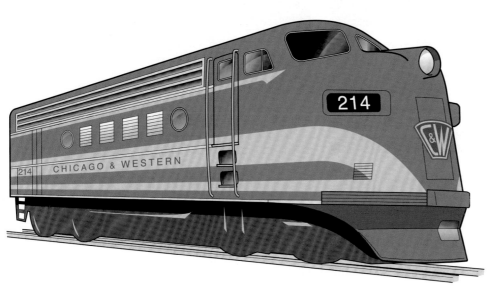

Fig. 5-6B: The Erie Lackawanna, Burlington, and Ontario & Western were three of several railroads that used the EMD "spear" stripe. Note that it is used "upside down" on the EL. The NYO&W unit (above, right) is an O scale All-Nation F3 superdetailed by the author in 1970.

styling department (fig. 5-9).

Dramatic color shifts can create a brand-new paint scheme. The Lake Superior & Ishpeming swapped green for red that's more fitting for an iron-ore carrier (fig 5-10).

Rolling stock graphics

Railroad sales and marketing departments as well as many shippers have long recognized that freight car sides can serve as moving billboards. In fact, billboard reefers were outlawed by the Interstate Commerce Commission in 1933 when it became apparent that less-well-heeled shippers were being forced to transport their products in cars that touted competitors' wares.

Slogans actually changed the name of at least one railroad. The Chicago, Indianapolis & Louisville told everyone it was the

Monon Route, a reflection of the Indiana town where its main lines crossed. The name became so closely associated with the railroad that in 1955 the reporting marks changed from CIL to MON. Obviously, shippers could more easily remember "Monon" or "The Hoosier Line" than the original name. (Monon, by the way, is pronounced "moe-non," not "mon-un.")

When I created the concept for the Allegheny Midland in 1973, I wanted it to have a name that, like the Monon, reflected its locale. I also wanted a colorful nickname that suggested its ties to the Nickel Plate Road. In hindsight, perhaps I should have chosen a longer corporate name such as Allegheny, Ohio & Western to justify a shorter nickname.

Before I settled on a herald

for my Allegheny Midland, I reviewed those used by other Appalachian coal haulers and finally drew one that has a lot of Norfolk & Western and Virginian characteristics (fig. 5-11). I confess that it also borrows from the Monon's wheel-on-rail herald; ignoring favorite railroads, even when they're in the wrong region, is difficult. Since that image creates a mixed message, perhaps I should have worked harder to adapt the NKP's square herald.

Nickel Plate Road graphics were used as a template for all Midland Road rolling stock (fig. 1-1). This spared me the potentially enormous task of creating painting and lettering diagrams and choosing colors for equipment ranging from cabooses to maintenance-of-way cars.

Like the NKP, which opted to use distinctive lettering in lieu of a herald, the AM used its herald sparingly. Only the NKP's Alco PA-1s, single GE 44-tonner, and piggyback trailers were emblazoned with the herald. The NKP's formal name—New York, Chicago & St. Louis—wasn't used on rolling stock, although "NYC&StL" was applied above the "NKP" reporting marks until World War II.

Allegheny Midland equipment was therefore lettered "Midland Road" with "AM" reporting marks, except for passenger cars, which got the more formal "Allegheny Midland" in an extended typeface. This isn't what the NKP did, but it worked for me.

I have a background as a drafter and could do the custom artwork for the Midland Road decal sets. This took some time, as I had to design letters, such as the M in Midland, to resemble the NKP typeface.

If you think your drawing skills aren't up to the task, I suggest you try this experiment before paying a custom-decal firm to do the artwork. Buy a pad of tracing paper with a light blue grid. Make a preliminary sketch of your proposed herald(s) eight times larger than the art will actually be printed on the decal sheet.

Play with the sketch until you have a design you like, then refine it a bit. Last, using a compass, circle template, and straightedge, or a very steady hand, make an even neater version of the sketch. Photocopy that pencil drawing on plain white paper and fill in the lines and letters

using a thin felt-tip pen. A personal-computer graphics package can also help you convert sketches into usable artwork.

Now here comes the neat part: Reduce your finished drawing back to scale size by making one or two reductions on the photocopier. You may find that your artwork looks just fine when reduced so much. If so, you've saved some money on your first order for custom decals. If not, it's worth the investment to have the art done, or redone, to the standards evident on the equipment and paper forms of a full-size railroad.

Rick Johnson reviewed the entire process in considerable detail in the March 2000 issue of *MR*. The example was Marty McGuirk's freelanced Southern New England, of the Canadian

Fig. 5-7: Variations of a classic EMD paint scheme have been used by railroads from coast to coast. The Conway Scenic RR in New Hampshire (bottom left) reprised it to celebrate the Boston & Maine and Maine Central schemes. Jack Ozanich photographed one of his freelanced Atlantic Great Eastern units in a version that's close to Lehigh Valley's original design (top). The LV later simplified the scheme with a single yellow stripe (bottom right, shown in February 1971).

Fig. 5-8: Wabash covered wagons originally wore an intricate combination of blue, white, and gray seen in 2001 on this F7 at the railroad museum in Monticello, Illinois. Like the LV, the Wabash saved money by shifting to a solid color with a yellow stripe that faintly echoed the old scheme.

Fig. 5-9: Bill Darnaby caught a meet between an L-1 Mountain and an E7 and E8 pair on a passenger train that shows off his HO scale Maumee's unique yet familiar EMD paint scheme. You've seen that nose treatment before, perhaps on Southern Fs and Es; the sides are similar to Wabash units.

National family with obvious Central Vermont overtones (fig. 5-12).

Lettering styles

There was once a time when typeface names like Helvetica, Copperplate Gothic, and Times Roman were known only to editors, art directors, and printers. Today everyone with a computer knows quite a few typefaces by sight. What you may not know can hurt you, however—or, more to the point, detract from the realism of your railroad.

The ever-popular Helvetica, for example, originated in Europe and migrated to North America in the early 1960s. Like many modern typefaces, it has

Fig. 5-12: Marty McGuirk photographed both Central Vermont and Southern New England steam power to show how he gives his freelanced HO models a CN-family appearance by using similar herald graphics and appropriate motive-power choices and detailing.

Fig. 5-10: Change the color and get a brand-new paint scheme, as the LS&I did on these two Alcos (left).

Fig. 5-11: The master artwork the author drew for Allegheny Midland passenger and freight units included extended NKP-style lettering for both AM and V&O passenger cars used in a Chicago-Newport News pool. Also shown is the herald for the short line Ridgeley & Midland County.

several distinctive characteristics that rarely showed up on older designs. Note, for example, the hooked (instead of straight) leg of a capital R, the flat bottom at the center of an M, and the long serif at the top of a numeral one:

R M 1

Using Helvetica for a 1950s railroad is therefore an obvious clanger, but such anachronisms are not hard to retouch using correcting fluid and a fine-tip marker.

Avant Garde, which Allen McClelland, Steve King, and I used when we combined our three freelanced railroads into the Appalachian Lines (cover photo and fig. 5-13), debuted around 1969. Our graphics folks must have

Fig. 5-13: Color panels and large Avant Garde lettering were used to give Appalachian Lines units a bold look. The three merged railroads (V&O and VM, shown here, and AM) retained their own colors but adopted an otherwise standard scheme.

gotten their hands on a pre-release sample, however, as it appeared on our rolling stock in January 1968.

To keep custom decal work to a minimum, you may be able to adapt commercial decal road numbers and graphics. You can even borrow road name decals by changing Northern Pacific to Pacific Northern, Southern Pacific to Pacific Southern, New York Central to Central New York, or Burlington Northern to North Burlington.

You may also be able to mask off a portion of a factory-painted model and airbrush in a different color for the body or a stripe. Think of a Baltimore & Ohio F unit with the blue above the black stripe and the color below changed to

maroon or green. Use low-tack masking tape to avoid peeling off the factory paint.

I expanded the Allegheny Midland's locomotive roster using commercial models painted for the Nickel Plate Road by scrubbing off the road name and number with a strong decal solvent and an eraser (I have since acquired a grit blaster, which can ease such chores) and applying Midland Road decals. This not only saved the cost and effort of applying the AM's NKP-style decal striping but also allowed me to letter units for which correct decal sets weren't available—Atlas Alco RS-11s and RSD-12s and Walthers FM switchers (fig. 1-7), for example.

Modern graphic trends

More modern diesel paint schemes often don't follow the graphic design standards in vogue when F units and early Geeps were delivered. A few traditional schemes survive, such as that of the Union Pacific, but most exhibit a more modern industrial design flavor—consider the Norfolk

Southern and the Guilford schemes. The BNSF scheme is more traditional with predecessor Great Northern overtones, but the resulting demise of the Santa Fe's classic red warbonnet livery (fig. 5-1) ended the reign of one of the best examples of railroad graphic design.

Today, almost anything goes as short lines create home-brewed paint schemes of varying quality. Some are money-saving adaptations of whatever livery a used locomotive arrived in (fig. 4-1); others strive to reflect the heritage of the region served by the railroad.

In any event, modelers of modern shortline railroads can hardly go wrong when creating a new paint scheme. The graphic design practices of the past are seldom observed, except when using a "heritage" paint scheme.

In some cases, echoes of the past are clearly seen. The CEO of the new Wheeling & Lake Erie is a former Rio Grande executive. Since the SP and then UP weren't using it, he brought the paint scheme with him (fig. 5-14). Other borrowed paint

schemes include those of the Detroit & Toledo Shore Line, the Algoma Central, and the Detroit Edison.

Migrating paint schemes

Some similar or even identical paint schemes resulted from mergers or equipment sales. The Rutland's green-and-yellow Alco-designed livery is a case in point. When that railroad was abandoned in 1961, portions of it became the Green Mountain (fig. 5-15) and the Vermont Railroads. The GMR retained the Rutland scheme and colors, whereas the VTR kept the end stripes but changed the colors to red and white. St. Johnsbury successor Lamoille Valley used a similar yellow scheme. The Tennessee Railroad acquired Rutland RS-1 400 and retained the green-and-yellow scheme for its fleet. I adopted the same approach for the Ridgeley & Midland County short line, which interchanged with the Allegheny Midland at Midland, West Virginia, by relettering Atlas Rutland RS-1s.

Choosing a name

One of the most evocative names for a freelanced railroad I can recall was the Great South Pass, which designer and former *MR* editor Linn Westcott applied to a track plan for a small layout. It didn't come close to fulfilling the grandeur conjured up by the name, creating an opportunity for someone to take that name and run with it. But what sort of railroad does "Great South Pass" suggest?

"Pass" denotes the West, as in White Pass & Yukon (fig. 1-9), Donner Pass, Cumbres Pass, and so on. (In the Northeast, a low point in a mountain chain is often called a notch, as in New Hampshire's Crawford Notch; to the south in central Appalachia, it's called a gap, as in Cumberland Gap. Somehow, Great South Notch or Great South Gap doesn't quite cut it.)

My vision for a Great South Pass Railroad is a line much like the Milwaukee Road's electrified Pacific Coast extension. It's a major player in the rail network, not some two-bit, one-horse outfit that barely ekes out a living. Its competitors are the likes of the Milwaukee Road, the Northern Pacific, and the Great Northern. Or maybe it's more like the Colorado Midland or a narrow-gauge pike of the Denver, South Park & Pacific's class that once had high hopes but probably wouldn't have survived World War II.

The herald and slogan should evoke lofty images of the American West and the pioneering spirit, of dreams that often exceed resources. The Union Pacific's shield herald and the Burlington's "Everywhere West" slogan set the right tone.

When choosing a name for a freelanced railroad, you should avoid names that were seldom used by full-size railroads, notably Transcontinental (sounds like a trucking company) and American (does the airline pop to mind?). Look instead for regional names that identify the railroad with a location. The names of states, cities, regions, and rivers, often coupled to a direction, are more typical of full-size railroads: Atlantic Coast Line, Western Pacific,

Fig. 5-14: Borrowed graphics are apparent in the Wheeling & Lake Erie's copy of the Rio Grande's scheme (top row). The NKP owned half of the Detroit & Toledo Shore Line, as its Geep paint scheme (middle left) shows. The Algoma Central's paint is a near copy of Erie Lackawanna's (middle right). Detroit Edison borrowed the EMD demonstrator scheme from the 1960s, even for its GE U-boats (bottom left). And tiny StJ&LC (bottom right) used striping much like that applied to the NKP's early Geeps, but upside down and partially in black against a red carbody.

Fig. 5-15: The original Rutland scheme is worn by successor Green Mountain's RS-1 no. 405 (right) at Rutland, Vermont, in 1972. The scheme migrated south to the Tennessee (below left, photo courtesy Max Robin). The Vermont Railway (below right), another successor, changed the colors and dropped the side stripes, as did the Lamoille Valley (bottom left). Relettering an Atlas Rutland RS-1 (bottom right) emulated prototype practices on the author's Ridgeley & Midland County.

Chicago Great Western, Wabash, Norfolk & Western, Pennsylvania, Texas & Pacific, Denver & Rio Grande Western, Maine Central, Lehigh Valley, and Virginian.

Allen McClelland's Virginian & Ohio, as opposed to Virginia & Ohio, is a nice touch. The name of Eric Brooman's Utah Belt is an interesting play on the Cotton Belt (St. Louis-Southwestern) and reflects his interest in the Southern

Pacific and its subsidiary. The Utah Belt's paint scheme seems right at home in the western mountains.

Before settling on Allegheny Midland, I made a list of regional names that I would consider using on my railroad, from Appalachian to Youghiogheny (pronounced "yuck-a-gheny"). I later discovered that Steve King went through the same process and rejected AM before settling on Virginia Midland. Obviously, this

process is subjective. But it's two against one, as John Wissinger predated both of us when he named a steam road that connected with his traction line the, you guessed it, Allegheny Midland.

Check old *Official Guides* (sold at railroadiana meets) for names that have fallen off the railroad mapscape due to abandonments or mergers and thus are ripe for reuse. The *Guide* also contains a list of every town and city served by a railroad, making it easier

to determine who your railroad's competitors will be as you refine its location.

Model photography

Before leaving the concept of creating an attractive, appropriate, and realistic image for your railroad, let's consider one more visual communication tool: model photography. With few exceptions, most highly regarded modelers "manage" the public image of their model railroads through

A herald for the I&StL

The development of a herald (with variations) for Mike Schafer's freelanced Illinois & St. Louis provides an interesting case study of the process.

Anyone familiar with the Steak 'n Shake restaurants will recognize the herald's heritage. During a food stop en route to a steam fan trip in 1970, Mike realized its potential as a model railroad graphic. It reminded him of the Southern Pacific's "ball and one wing" herald used on *Daylight*-era passenger equipment and the Erie's circle-in-diamond-with wings artwork; the nose of Virginian electrics also sported a similar design.

The logo went through a series of iterations, as shown below. When Mike met with Ron Roberts of Rail Graphics to discuss custom decals, Ron observed that the italicized slogan inside the inner circle would be hard to "hold"–print clearly. The slogan was then replaced with a large "I" as a salute to the railroad's home state. The Bookman Demi serif typeface used for the railroad's name was also changed to sans-serif ITC Kabel, a type popularized during the Art Deco movement in the 1920s.

Two more variations came about because the ampersand (&) seemed to intrude on the "St. Louis" lettering. Friends Craig Willett, an Amtrak engineer, and Darin Umlauft of the Walthers product-development department offered Mike some sage advice.

Mike now had a herald, but no route had been defined for the railroad. He reviews the process of determining his route in a sidebar in chapter 7.

Fig. 5-16: A Midland Road Mikado pounds by the wood depot at Gap Run, Virginia. Model photos cropped to eliminate distractions such as the fascia and aisle help to establish a sense of realism beyond the models themselves.

carefully considered and composed photographs of their layouts.

I found that photos of the Allegheny Midland also became important to me in that they created a sense of realism that the models themselves could not. The photographs were cropped to eliminate distractions, such as aisles, fascias, and poor viewing angles, and they disguised the models' scale. The photos showed the railroad in a realistic manner, most often from the vantage point of a scale height person standing at trackside.

Thanks to an image shot for an *MR* cover, Gap Run, Virginia, became not just a short stretch of track between two tunnel portals at the end of an aisle but rather a small town in the Appalachians served by the Allegheny Midland. An AM Mikado blasting by the depot in a photo (fig. 5-16) looked more realistic than it did during an operating session.

Mounting photos of prototype scenes on a valance or fascia near each modeled or to-be-modeled scene is helpful. Even if you're freelancing, viewers can learn a great deal about your objectives from such photos, which serve as reminders about future scenery plans.

You can also impose a sense of history by setting up photos that show the same scene at an earlier time. If your railroad depicts the 1970s, for example, you could model the foundations of a since-demolished depot or water tower (fig. 4-8) along the right-of-way.

Temporarily moving a structure from another location on the layout, or quickly assembling an inexpensive plastic kit on top of the foundation and posing some vintage equipment in front of it will make a fine portrait of your railroad in an earlier period. You may get such photos printed in black and-white to suggest an era before color photography became common.

Thanks to digital cameras, photography is becoming an increasingly important aspect of model railroading. We should continuously look at our layouts through a viewfinder to ensure that we include features that enhance their appearance in photos and eliminate those that detract.

CHAPTER SIX
Creating a roster

Fig. 6-1: The Allegheny Midland Mikado and Railway Post Office car needed only new Nickel Plate Road lettering to be at home on the author's new NKP layout, but the Wheeling & Lake Erie-style steel caboose never made it onto the NKP's St. Louis Division.

Tempting as it is to buy one of these and one of those, the process of building a roster of locomotives and cars benefits from the same sort of analysis used to choose a railroad and era to model. With some notable exceptions, for example, I found that only a few of the locomotives and cars used on my freelanced 1957 Appalachian coal hauler (fig. 6-1) are suitable for reuse on my new layout, the NKP St. Louis Division, which depicts a prototype granger line in Indiana and Illinois in 1954. Just a few years and less than a thousand miles make a big difference.

Fig. 6-2: The Duluth, Missabe & Iron Range's fleet of articulateds and six-motor diesels (photographed in 1984) lugged ore jimmies between the unloading piers in Duluth, Minnesota, and the pits. Such action can keep many crewmembers busy loading ore boats against a tight shipping schedule. The paint scheme matches the cargo: iron ore.

Tough choices

Choosing a region and era to model may depend heavily upon roster preferences. Those modelers who enjoy seeing long strings of ore jimmies (fig. 6-2) or coal hoppers will choose a different prototype or base railroad than those who want to run strings of "yellow bellies" (refrigerator cars) or "high cars" (boxcars).

Locomotive preferences also weigh heavily when it comes to the choice of a prototype, era, and even scale and gauge. Modeling a specific railroad at a favorite time and place requires that the needed motive power be attainable at an affordable price.

The diesel era brought with it relatively standardized carbodies that give modelers a common starting point for railroad-specific detailing projects. You may have to swap exhaust fans and stacks, add or delete headlights and dynamic brakes, and modify the fuel tank configuration to match your railroad's diesel fleet, but all of that is part of what sets your railroad apart.

Most modelers can tell an EMD GP9 from a GP35 or an Alco Century 420 from a C-636 (fig. 6-3). For those

of you modeling the steam era, however, it may appear that every railroad had unique steam locomotives—certainly nothing that was the equivalent of the seemingly ubiquitous EMD F unit or Geep. But there were some interesting cases of steam locomotives with a common heritage.

The most obvious example is the United States Railway Administration (USRA) series of locomotives dating from World War I. Little good came out of the government's wartime takeover of the nation's railroads, but the USRA's steam designs were a notable exception. The series embraced 0-6-0 and 0-8-0 switchers, light and heavy Pacifics (4-6-2s), Mikados (2-8-2s), Mountains (4-8-2s), and Santa Fes (2-10-2s) as well as articulated 2-6-6-2 and 2-8-8-2 Mallets.

The wide distribution of USRA locomotives enables many prototype modelers to re-create a favorite railroad's roster. Similarly, it gives freelancers a head start in creating rosters that support almost any type of "modern" steam railroading.

Using a standardized

design does not mean that your railroad will necessarily look like everyone else's. It's amazing how a few cosmetic changes can drastically alter a locomotive's appearance. The USRA light Mikados shown in fig. 6-4 illustrate how the addition of an Elesco feedwater heater atop the smokebox, illuminated number boards and a Mars light on the smokebox front, stack extension, and different tenders, among other details, give each of these NKP Mikes a different look.

John Swanson applied these appliance detailing principles to his freelanced Dixon, Wyanet & Lake Superior's steam fleet. John's admiration of the Chicago, Burlington & Quincy's steam operations is evident in the DW&LS, a midwestern granger line set in the 1920s, whose locomotives exhibit several CB&Q characteristics, notably the Elesco feedwater heater ahead of the stack, high-mounted headlight, and jaunty cab (fig. 6-5).

Tenders are one of the easiest details to change, fostering not only a distinctive appearance but also complementing a locomotive's usage. The NKP

lengthened 12,000-gallon USRA tenders to hold 16,000 gallons and even had Lima build a series of 20,000-gallon tenders for many of its USRA light Mikes to stretch the engines' range (fig. 6-4). With good firing, a skilled hand at the throttle, and a bit of luck, runs crossing over an entire division without a water stop became practical.

But such changes had consequences. Short turntables from the era of Consolidations (2-8-0s) and Ten-Wheelers (4-6-0s) couldn't accommodate Mikes, Mountains, and Berkshires with long tenders. Some railroads specified short tenders on otherwise modern locomotives (fig. 5-12), thus restricting their range, while others

Fig. 6-3: Alco heaven—a Century 420 in the post-1959 scheme idles beside a C-636 in Appalachian Lines paint and an RS-11 in the as-delivered scheme at the AM engine terminal in Sunrise, Virginia.

installed longer turntables.

Longer tenders were heavier, so in many cases bridges had to be strengthened or replaced. Even roundhouse stalls often had to be extended or new stalls built. The choice of a tender could thus move the railroad's era past the time when the old roundhouse you hoped to model was scrapped or modernized.

Borrowed designs

In addition to the widespread usage of the standardized USRA designs, there are examples of steam locomotive designs that were shared by two or more railroads. This was due to a variety of factors, such as the control of one railroad by another or the move of an official from one railroad to another.

For example, when two Chesapeake & Ohio officials went to the Virginian, it wasn't long before near

copies of the C&O's Super-Power 2-8-4s and incredible 2-6-6-6s appeared on VGN rails. The 2-8-4s already had a multi-railroad heritage in that they were designed by the Advisory Mechanical Committee, a joint venture of railroads owned by the Van Sweringen brothers of Cleveland: NKP, C&O, Pere Marquette, and Erie. The NKP, PM, and C&O 2-8-4s were scaled-down versions of the AMC-developed C&O class T-1 2-10-4 (fig. 6-6). The Richmond, Fredericksburg & Potomac also bought near-duplicates. Their similar designs offer considerable cost savings to model manufacturers.

AMC influence even extended to the fiercely independent Pennsylvania RR. When the PRR needed big power during World War II, it tested C&O T-1 and Norfolk & Western class A 2-6-6-4 locomotives. The

T-1 impressed PRR officials, and they built J1 and J1a classes of these huge Texas types. Changing the front-end treatment, cab windows, and tender gave this AMC design a distinct Pennsy look (fig. 6-6), a lesson for freelancers looking for ways to give "stock" locomotives a family appearance.

We tend to think of off-the-shelf models as being artifacts of the diesel era, but Baldwin, for one, offered a wide range of almost stock models. The stock Baldwin 4-6-0 (fig. 6-7), recently reproduced in two versions by Bachmann, is a good example of "plain vanilla" steam power from around the turn of the 20th century used on a variety of railroads large and small. Two other excellent "stock" model steam engines are the Bachmann (N and HO) and Weaver (O) 2-8-0, which has 62″ rather than the more common 57″ drivers, but is

still a good base model. With all of these options available, building a convincing freelanced roster without investing in brass is as practical for those modeling the steam era as it is for those who favor diesels.

Will they do the job?

There's one other major consideration when choosing an era, assuming the needed locomotives are available and affordable in your preferred scale: Will they do the job? You may be fond of Camelback Ten-Wheelers, for example, and be able to afford the brass imports thereof for your chosen railroad and era. But do they have enough tractive effort to pull passenger or freight trains of reasonable length on level track, let alone up any grades (including helixes) you may have planned? If not, is there room to add weight? Can you handle or afford to job out such work?

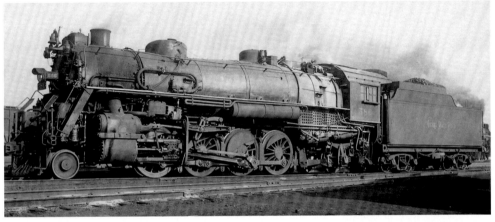

Fig. 6-4: These portraits of NKP USRA light Mikados show how details affect appearance. A 1940s photo (left) from Howard W. Ameling shows ex-Lake Erie & Western H-6o no. 586 with a Hodges trailing truck, Worthington Type S feedwater heater, air compressors on the pilot deck, and short original tender. Richard Donelson photographed USRA copy H-6e 643 (above left) in October 1947 sporting a Delta trailing truck, Elesco feedwater heater, illuminated number boards, compressors and feedwater pump on the left side, and Berkshire-style tender. H-6e 639 (above right, shot by Don Wood in July 1956) lost its feedwater heater and has deck-mounted pumps, Mars light, extended stack, and stretched USRA tender with a Buckeye front truck and an Andrews at rear.

Consider the cars that such locomotives will be asked to pull. If your passenger trains are brass imports, they're likely to be heavy. Can that high-stepping American (4-4-0), Atlantic (4-4-2), or Pacific (4-6-2) lug them around your layout at a reasonable speed? Can your favorite 2-8-0, 2-8-2, or 2-10-0 pull long trains of loaded hoppers or ore jimmies to lake or tidewater ports?

Rich Weyand models the Norfolk & Western in N scale, and he found that, unlike their prototypes, an A- or Y-class articulated model could not pull as many hoppers as a three-unit diesel model could. He solved this problem by taking advantage of the N&W's practice of coupling a canteen (second tender filled with water) behind the locomotive. He slightly extended a canteen shell to fit over a diesel chassis,

then had several additional shells cast in resin. As Rich described in *Model Railroad Planning 2002*, this "booster" added enough tractive effort to match the articulateds' performance to the diesels'.

The wide range of steam locomotive kits from Bowser, Model Die Casting (fig. 6-5), and other manufacturers offers ways to acquire a sizable steam fleet at modest cost and effort. Railroad-specific details, even the square-shouldered Belpaire fireboxes favored by the Pennsylvania, can be filed off to create more generic boilers.

Freight car choices

Many modelers spend as much time checking what's behind the locomotive in railroad photos as they do looking at the motive power. Overviews of yards are valuable as the historians among us try to determine what freight car types and

road names appeared in various regions and in what proportion to home-road cars.

The master modelers who create patterns for resin car kits are also students of traffic patterns, and they strive to create models of cars that are at once relatively common yet unlikely to be mass-produced in plastic. Thanks to one-piece body shells, the task of assembling many resin kits has become a pleasant pastime that's within the capabilities of most modelers.

Some roster choices will be made for us when we choose a specific part of a prototype railroad or locate our freelanced railroads in a specific region. A railroad set in the Pacific Northwest, for example, would earn a lot of revenue from the movement of lumber and paper products. Lumber would typically move in boxcars and flatcars back in the

steam era; today it would be loaded onto center-beam flats and transported.

Paper continues to be shipped in boxcars. Kaolin, a clay used to make porcelain bathroom fixtures as well as to coat "enameled" paper, was once shipped as a dry powder in boxcars equipped with roof hatches (fig. 6-8). Now it's shipped as a slurry in tank cars, some clearly marked as to their contents. Such models are commercially

Fig. 6-5: John Swanson's free-lanced Dixon, Wyanet & Lake Superior steam locomotives, with their high-mounted headlights, Elesco feedwater heaters, and jaunty cabs, draw inspiration from neighbor Burlington (below). John kitbashed this small Mikado from a Model Die Casting 2-8-0 mechanism and an ATSF 2-6-2 boiler. (CB&Q photo by Ken Oltera.)

available, and they make it easier for crews switching paper mills to know which car goes where: the roof-hatch-equipped box or the tank car that says KAOLIN in big letters goes on the kaolin track.

Similarly, the Thrall-Door all-door boxcar, offered in HO by Life-Like and Walthers, is available with lettering that all but yells its contents at observers: "U.S. Plywood" and "Masonite" are two examples. Since these cars are closed, you can use them as loads or empties without having to remove a coal load from a hopper or machinery from a flatcar.

Having a car's lading indicated so clearly is helpful with "virtual" industries. You can simulate a large plant by running a spur from your main behind a building or some trees, or even off the edge of the benchwork, without modeling the factory. Since crews can't see what's not modeled, it helps to give them visual clues as to the type of industry they're theoretically setting cars out for or picking cars up from. This is easily done by using cars that obviously contain a specific product.

Realism vs. durability

As I illustrated on page 41 of *Realistic Model Railroad Operation*, our desire for more realistic models has to be balanced against the likelihood of damage to delicate details during operating sessions. Often as you lecture visiting crewmembers about not picking up your models when they're trying to uncouple them, damage will occur when cars are sideswiped or someone snags an uncoupling tool on a ladder or cut lever.

Operating sessions have a dual purpose: We want to re-create some aspect of full-size railroading in a realistic manner, and we want to enjoy doing so. As hosts of operating sessions, we have an obligation to tell everyone what we expect of them and our railroads, and we should do our best to ensure that they have a good time.

If we're constantly on their backs about not damaging equipment or scenery, we'll create enough tension to spoil the fun. On the other hand, if we have crewmembers that don't seem to understand our objectives and get with the program, it may be time to find others who do.

Cabooses

As with steam engines, there used to be little standardization among railroads when it came to caboose design. You could tell railroads apart as easily by their cabooses as by their depots. If your favorite railroad's standard caboose or something similar (fig. 6-9) isn't available commercially, you may be facing a major kitbashing or scratchbuilding project. With luck, you may find something close that can serve as a stand-in until time for such projects is more abundant.

The chore facing a freelancer is to build up a standardized caboose roster with a readily available

Fig. 6-6: What a difference details make: PRR J1 2-10-4 no. 6490 (left) is mechanically "identical" to C&O T-1 no. 3036 (below), but the J1's cab, front end, and tender give it a Pennsy look. Similar easy-to-make changes on model locomotives can create a family appearance. (PRR photo by C.W. Jernstom; C&O photo by G.G. Grabill Jr.)

caboose that's appropriate for the region or base prototype. Fortunately, many railroads used the "Northeastern" steel caboose bought in quantity by the Western Maryland (fig. 6-10), the Reading, and many other lines, and which has since migrated all over the map. Life-Like's model of this caboose would be a good choice for many freelancers.

The passenger fleet

Like cabooses, passenger cars tended to be railroad-specific. In recent years, however, a diverse fleet of passenger car types representing various builders has become available, and companies such as New England Rail Service offer detail parts that allow us to modify existing kits into a variety of prototypically accurate models.

Passenger trains usually reflected the scope and financial health of a railroad. The Santa Fe's fleet of passenger trains running between Chicago and Los Angeles carried movie stars and the like, and their glittering stainless exteriors reflected that glamour. Both the New York Central's fleet, conservatively dressed in its gray pinstriped "suits," and the Pennsy's sedate Tuscan

red livery were clearly associated with the Big Apple. Several carriers in the South and the West sported flamboyant schemes hinting at the sun and fun that awaited vacationers in the warmer climes they served.

Smaller railroads tried hard to convince potential customers that they, too, were

as modern and up-to-date as their much larger brethren. The perennially poor New York, Ontario & Western hired stylist Otto Kuhler of Milwaukee Road *Hiawatha* fame to use paint and a modicum of sheet metal to upgrade its *Mountaineer* and the 4-8-2 that pulled it.

Itinerant railroad executive

Fig. 6-7: Perennial favorite Maryland & Pennsylvania operated a small fleet of stock Baldwin 2-8-0s and 4-6-0s. Until recently, Ma & Pa modelers had only one option: brass imports, such as this Pacific Fast Mail Ten-Wheeler. Bachmann now offers such Baldwin classics in affordable plastic.

Fig. 6-8: Specialized cars, such as this V&O kaolin boxcar, help identify a railroad's traffic base and region. Unlike hoppers and flatcars, "closed-load" cars don't need to have their loads removed between operating sessions to simulate empties.

Fig. 6-9: Clinchfield's end-cupola cabooses are near twins of a standard Santa Fe design. Allen McClelland took advantage of this to create a plausible caboose fleet at low cost using Athearn's ATSF caboose kits.

John Barriger brought new life to Monon passenger trains at bargain prices by acquiring steam-boiler-equipped EMD F3s and army hospital cars, which shop forces rebuilt into what appeared to be modern streamlined trains (fig. 6-11). They were initially painted red, white, and gray, a nod to on-line Indiana University's colors, with the freight units painted in rival Purdue's black and gold, but eventually everything got the latter colors. Chicago & Eastern Illinois embraced the blue and orange of the University of Illinois, so this is a plausible way for freelancers to select colors for their railroads (fig. 5-1B).

Our preferences for freight or passenger trains sway our choices of prototypes. In fact, the main theme of your railroad may be passenger service. Instead of a freight classification yard, you may opt for a union station with switchers cutting off and adding cars as trains originate, terminate, or pass through.

This decision affects layout design. Full-length passenger cars, especially those equipped with diaphragms and coupled a scale distance apart, look much better on curves of 36″ or larger in HO. Backing passenger trains through sharp turnouts (no. 6s are barely adequate) or running through crossovers sharper than no. 8s is often problematic or unrealistic (fig. 6-13).

Another concern with long passenger cars (or modern auto racks, high-cube boxcars, Trailer Train flats, or double-stacks) is that their overhang may foul trains on an adjacent curved yard or passing track. I found that using a 30″ radius on the main and a 32″ radius on an adjacent passing track was pushing my luck with big articulated locomotives (fig. 6-14). Recently released articulateds from several makers are built to handle relatively sharp curves.

Open loads

Open cars, such as hoppers, flatcars, and gondolas, present layout design challenges. If you shove a loaded hopper into a power plant, for example, it will still be loaded when it comes time to pick up that car. This problem can be handled between operating sessions by reverse-switching the railroad—running the loads back to the coal mines or to an interchange with a coal-originating railroad, and running the empty

hoppers from staging or a coal mine back to the power plant. This will take time, but you get to run your railroad by yourself, which often uncovers problems crews failed to report.

A more elegant solution using "paired industries" was proposed years ago by John Armstrong. He located a coal preparation plant on one side of a backdrop and a power plant on the other. The tracks into the plant directly connected to those under the coal tipple. When you shoved loaded hoppers into the power plant, they

Fig. 6-10: The "Northeastern" caboose was used by many railroads, including the Western Maryland (seen on Helmstetter's Curve near Cumberland, Maryland, in May 1973). These popular cabooses migrated to many short lines, including the New Hope & Ivyland in Pennsylvania.

Fig. 6-11: Even smaller railroads, such as the Monon, took pride in their passenger fleet. Number 6, leaving Lafayette, Indiana, in August 1967 behind a C-420, has two coaches rebuilt from army hospital cars.

Fig. 6-14: John Armstrong's paired-industries scheme allows loaded hoppers to be shoved into a power plant and reappear on the other side of a central backdrop as loads coming out of a coal mine. On this On2½ plan by Chris Webster, empties are shoved into a mine and come out of a coal prep plant, a consequence of cleaned coal being loaded into standard-gauge hoppers.

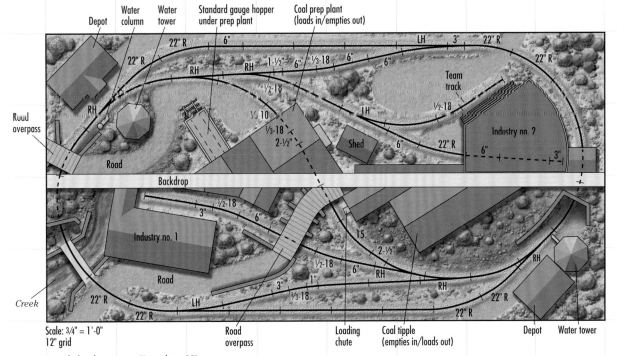

Scale: 3/4" = 1'-0"
12" grid

Unmarked track sections are 9" straights or 18" curves.
All turnouts are Custom-Line no. 4's.

Fig. 6-12: These two photos (right) show the improvement in train dynamics when full-length passenger cars negotiate a no. 8 (left) instead of a no. 6 crossover.

Fig. 6-13: A scratchbuilt WM 4-6-6-4 owned by Max Robin gave the crew of an AM PA-1 a great view of its smokebox front as it negotiated a 30″ curve (below left). The AM's 2-6-6-2s looked better on those curves (below right).

magically appeared to be rolling out from under the prep plant's conveyors. When you pulled those loads forward to the power plant and replaced them with empties, it appeared that empty hoppers were rolling out of the power plant. Figure 6-11 shows how Chris Webster applied this idea to a 4- by 8-foot On2½ layout, described on page 26 of *Model Railroad Planning 2002*.

Numbering equipment

When I created a roster for AM locomotives and cars, including cabooses and maintenance-of-way cars, I initially based it on the Nickel Plate's roster. If the NKP numbered hoppers in the 30000 series, so did I. I had to find new slots for car types, such as wood-chip and pulpwood cars that the NKP didn't have.

When numbering AM locomotives, I tried to use gaps in the NKP's locomotive roster to avoid duplications. This worked well at times— my Berkshires were numbered 780–799 behind NKP 700–779, for example—but I soon found that some overlap was inevitable, especially for the diesel roster.

When Allen McClelland, Steve King, and I merged our railroads into the

Appalachian Lines, we adopted horsepower-based numbers for locomotives. A 2,000-hp GP38 was numbered in the 2000 series. The 3000 series quickly became filled, so some 3,000-hp units migrated to the 3100 series.

It's helpful to create a standard form for a three-ring binder that you can fill out to cover each type of car and locomotive on your roster. The form should list the car type and number series as well as the model used to build it—an Atlas RS-3 or an Athearn twin hopper, for example, including the manufacturer's kit number. To avoid duplicates, be sure to record every car and locomotive number as you add them. Write down the source of all detail parts and decals as well as the paint brand and color and weathering techniques

used on each model so you can copy your initial example when adding rolling stock to the roster.

Making reasonable choices

It's easy to be overwhelmed by today's plethora of choices. You may find yourself reading the fine print on the kits to be sure you don't buy a boxcar built in 1955 for your 1954 railroad.

Such concerns can add interest to the hobby if you're far enough along the path toward an operating model railroad to have time to cope with details. But they can also get in your way if you develop analysis paralysis and don't buy anything that isn't certified by the Perfectly Correct Police as being ideal for your railroad.

Building a model railroad is an endless series of compromises. Never compromise on the quality of

Additional reading

These articles are of considerable value when you're building up your locomotive or rolling stock fleet:
• "Freight car pooling" by Bob Davis and Larry DeYoung, *Railroad Model Craftsman*, April 1983, pp. 76–81.
• "Locomotives of the Maumee Route" by Bill Darnaby, *Model Railroader*, May 1991, pp. 64–71.
• "Upgrade your freight car fleet" by John Nehrich, *Model Railroader*, December 1991, pp. 140–43.

framework and track because they're hard to upgrade later. But feel free to cut corners when doing so will help you reach your objectives sooner without compromising long-term goals.

CHAPTER SEVEN

Geography and scenery

The difference between generic scenery and structures and those that reflect a slice of reality can be remarkable. Visitors immediately connect with familiar scenes (fig. 7-1), and their knowledge influences how they perceive the modeled scene (fig. 3-8). If what they see is in synch with their memories or expectations, then a model seems more realistic.

By the same token, knowledgeable viewers associate certain "signature" scenes and types of structures with specific regions: grain elevators with the Great Plains and mills with New England, for example. Using such archetypical cues is akin to posting a sign identifying the location and type of railroad being modeled on your layout.

Fig. 7-1: QN Cabin at Quinnimont, West Virginia, on the Chesapeake & Ohio (now CSX) became famous for its "depot-plus-tower" yardmaster's office. Was the author's decision to "borrow" such a well-known scene for use on his Allegheny Midland (fig. 3-8) a wise choice?

Fig. 7-2: Signature structures, such as this brick mill and wood-frame machine shop in Winchendon, Massachusetts, can silently tell a detailed story about the location, purpose, and era of a model railroad.

Fig. 7-3: This truck-dump tipple at Trammel, Virginia, on the Clinchfield (below left), can be kitbashed using parts from a Walthers mine kit (below right).

Signature structures

It's usually easier to build a convincing structure or scene when you follow a prototype's example. Only a few of us are gifted architects or artists, able to conjure up plausible buildings and scenery at will. Too often the rest of us create fanciful interpretations that look like theme-park sets in the eyes of knowledgeable observers.

As we look at business or residential districts, especially in older towns, we should keep an eye out for those that typify the region, as opposed to the eye-catchers. That said, I confess that I've been in New England towns where every structure seemed

to be a jaw-dropper (fig. 7-2). Though that may not be typical, including several such structures on your layout instead of one showstopper would suggest they are bona fide traffic sources for a railroad instead of merely modeling spectacles.

Coal tipples (fig. 7-3) and company stores and towns are good examples of "signature" structures in Appalachia. But company towns aren't restricted to the coalfields. Where I live in northwestern New Jersey, at least an hour from hard-coal country in northeastern Pennsylvania, there are rows of company houses near former shoe factories and textile mills.

Nearby may be the remnants of a company store (fig. 7-4), a convenience to workers as well as a symbol of the days when workers were paid in company-issued scrip that could be redeemed for goods only at that store.

A number of signature industries can help viewers understand the purpose of a railroad and the region it serves. These include steel mills (fig. 7-5), pulpwood yards, logging camps, grain elevators (fig. 7-6), canning plants, brickyards (fig. 7-7), cement plants, tidewater port facilities (fig. 7-8), paper mills (fig. 7-9), gravel pits and rock quarries, power plants, auto and truck plants, perishable-

loading areas, textile mills, home-appliance factories, breweries and distilleries, ore stamping mills, chemical plants, tire factories, and glass-making plants.

It's hard to look at magazine ads and model railroad catalogs without coming across structure kits that appeal to our model-building instincts. But some industries represented by kits are too small to alone support rail service in the 20th or 21st century. Many modelers are nonetheless tempted to seek operational variety by scattering such mini-industries around the layout.

A more plausible approach

Fig. 7-4: Where there are mines, company stores and houses aren't far away. Company stores featured both wood (top left) and brick (below) construction. The walls from two Pikestuff kits were combined to make an HO model (bottom left) of a typical brick structure. A row of company houses (bottom right) adds realism to a coal-hauling railroad; these were kitbashed from "Ma's Place" stores.

may be to select one large industry that receives a wide variety of car types. Consider a paper mill. Finished paper is often shipped as huge rolls or cardboard sheets in watertight boxcars. Inbound traffic is far more varied. Mills receive wood pulp in the form of wood chips in extended-top or "oversized" open hoppers or as pulpwood logs on special flatcars. They may receive dried kaolin to coat or "fill" the paper in boxcars with roof hatches or, more recently, in tank cars as slurry. (It's now cheaper to pay the shipping charges for the extra weight of the water than to pay for heat to dry the clay, and the paper mill needs to add water to dried kaolin anyway.)

Paper mill powerhouses use fuel, which comes in hoppers (coal) or tank cars (oil). Chlorine in tank cars is needed to bleach some types of paper, and kraft mills need odoriferous chemicals to dissolve wood pulp. Some mills bring in cardboard (chemical pulp) from other operations and mix it with wood pulp to strengthen their paper.

You need not model all of such a large industry to gain a big operational advantage. Building only one or a few representative structures between the main line and the aisle will announce its presence. Then build one long lead track that goes "into the plant" and is truncated at the edge of the benchwork. (Running the industrial lead behind a hill or large structure near the backdrop works equally well.)

Fig. 7-5: Thanks to Walthers, modeling a steel mill is no longer a massive scratchbuilding project. Everything behind the first row of buildings could be a photo mural. Bernie Kempinski photo.

Fig. 7-6: "Sentinels of the prairies" punctuate the flat midwestern landscape and come in all shapes and sizes in a variety of materials. The electrified Fort Dodge, Des Moines & Southern served these two grain elevators in Boone, Iowa (below left).

Achieving a balance

How does the freelancer evoke a specific region without copying a specific prototype? Bill Darnaby took a typical midwestern depot design and modified its siding and trim to create a standard depot for his HO scale Maumee that looks familiar yet is unique. Bill scratchbuilt his depots; an alternative is to use an inexpensive generic kit, such as the Walthers Trainline depot (fig. 7-10).

Bill also created place names that sounded similar to, but were not clones of, actual towns in Ohio—Sciotovale instead of Sciotoville, for example. The only town on the Maumee that he named for and modeled after an actual site is Edison. There, Bill

superimposed the Maumee's main on an actual junction between two New York Central System lines to create a three-way crossing (fig. 7-11), as he described in the 2004 issue of *Model Railroad Planning*.

Keeping geology in mind

Knowing where your prototype or freelanced railroad fits on a map is a major step toward realism. Viewers can usually tell at a glance what part of the continent a railroad serves by looking at rock formations, rivers, plains, and even crops. If you build generic scenery, communication and, hence, realism often suffer.

After all, before building or detailing a model of a railroad-specific caboose or locomotive, most of us would

try to locate scale drawings and detail photos. We might wing it when it comes to building a freelanced depot, but we'd keep in mind common depot architecture.

Yet we often launch into far larger and more significant projects— like scenicking the railroad— without doing any homework. That the resulting landforms are too generic to depict a given region isn't surprising. It probably harkens back to the hobby's formative years when modelers were too busy building craftsman kits and getting the railroad running to worry about its location on the map or the associated specifics of scenery.

We all have areas of keen interest and specialization, but that does not excuse us

from trying to create a setting for our railroads that is as realistic and attentive to detail as the structures and rolling stock they surround. The most accurate boxcar model will lose much of its visual impact if it's rolling on shiny track looped around a Ping-Pong table.

Scenery gaffs often arise in a subtle manner, however. When my wife and I bought our first basement— uh, house—I designed a freelanced railroad for it. I should have dubbed it the Smorgasbord Central, as it had one of everything: mountain range, ocean port, coal mine, grain elevator, long and curving timber trestle, you name it. The only thing I left out was the town of Plausibility.

I still have no idea where

Fig. 7-7: Brickyards, like this one managed by the author's father in Cayuga, Indiana, shipped brick in boxcars and received fuel to fire the kilns in hoppers or tank cars. Mr. Plaster products make them easy to model.

Fig. 7-8: Joe Greenstein gets credit for this informative portrait of railroading along the waterfront. The New York Cross Harbor Alco switcher rides on the tug-powered car float because there's no locomotive on the New Jersey side.

rocks, including bituminous (soft) coal, which have been uplifted but not badly folded.

Selecting a segment to model

Selecting a prototype refines your focus, but you still need to select a specific segment of it to model. Think beyond the scenic possibilities; a towering trestle is fun to build and then watch trains tiptoe across—for a while. But watching trains navigate through scenery grows tiresome, so it pays to find a railroad segment that offers interesting operation as well as an attractive setting. Once the trains start operating realistically, the action tends to redirect our attention from the scenery to the work at hand.

The focus on what a railroad does, as opposed to the scenery it traverses or the equipment it operates, has opened up layout design options. The granger roads of the Midwest, for example, cross seemingly endless and featureless prairies as they gather farm products and haul bridge traffic between connecting lines. But why would anyone want to model the flatlands? Frequent interchanges, for one thing, as I'll discuss in chapter 8.

the railroad was supposed to be located or what it did for a living. What saved me from spending too much time and money on that rudderless vessel was a number of field trips to Appalachia and a growing familiarity with the principles embodied in my friend Allen McClelland's freelanced Virginian & Ohio.

What I observed on Allen's model railroad didn't match what I had planned for my layout, and the original concept, I'm happy to say, died when we built our present home. By then, I had gained enough knowledge to create a more

plausible concept for the Allegheny Midland.

A key difference was that the AM was located on a map, as discussed in the following section. This, in turn, nailed down its raison d'être and defined its scenery. My studies of geology that grew out of researching the Appalachian landscape became a secondary hobby and consistently make travel more interesting.

Whether the rocks along our railroad will be flat or folded sediments, columnar cliffs of basalt, or barren granite summits rounded by glacial ice or unrelenting rain and wind depends on where

it is located. Thus, we should be able to tell a lot about a freelanced railroad's location by looking at its scenery.

The collision of the African and North American plates hundreds of millions of years ago lifted and folded rocks east of a "hinge line" that extends through central Pennsylvania and south along the eastern border of West Virginia. That's why there's anthracite (hard) coal in northeastern Pennsylvania; the unrelenting heat and pressure resulting from the collision drove out the impurities. West of that line in the Appalachian Plateau, we expect to see sedimentary

Fig. 7-9: The Claremont Electric Railway once switched the far side of this small, picturesque paper mill in Claremont, New Hampshire. Note the green-painted mullions, typical of many red brick buildings. An old Revell enginehouse kit with pilasters added might make a good starting point.

Consider such a railroad in terms of a multi-level layout design. It's difficult to model tall, deep scenes on such layouts, because the upper level isn't all that far above the lower—typically 12" to 18" (fig. 7-12). The bad news is that it's hard to build sweeping scenic vistas on the lower deck. The good news is that you don't need to if you model a granger line.

Railroads in the farm belt typically have rights-of-way 100 feet or so in width, often marked with fences. A hundred feet in HO is about 14", and many multi-level layouts are built on shelves about that wide. That allows room for the fence lines, a row of trees, and a pole line along them, which help to obscure the close-at-hand sky backdrop. A photo mural of a distant farm every 10 feet or so along the backdrop completes the scene (fig. 7-13). And you don't have to cope with modeling acres of corn or soybeans or wheat; to a large extent, they're "in the aisle."

If you'd like to model a coal road and aren't sure where coalfields were located, a visit to a library will help. (Also see the coal map on page 20 of *Realistic Model Railroad Operations*.) Industrial directories, such as the annual *Keystone Coal Industry Manual* (McGraw-Hill), which also lists cement plants, are helpful. The Operations Special Interest Group of the NMRA (www.opsig.com) maintains an industry database and issues an informative magazine, the *Dispatcher's Office*.

Putting the railroad on a map

On page 66, Mike Schafer explains how he created a plausible route map for his freelanced HO granger railroad, the Illinois & St. Louis. He thought about how the railroad might gain a competitive edge by bypassing Chicago, a well-known bottleneck. Mike picked actual town names to give the mythical line a ring of truth, and modeled recognizable features (Caterpillar's plant in East Peoria and State Line interlocking, for example).

Similarly, when plotting a course for the AM, I first consulted a railroad atlas to find routes that were not as yet, or were no longer, served by rail. This is a perilous quest, as there are good reasons why no rails grace those paths, but it's an interesting exercise nonetheless. Step two was to take a closer look using large highway maps of each state.

Then came the most interesting exercise of all: I purchased U.S. Geological Survey topographical "quadrangle" maps for the proposed route and drew a line representing the railroad. These maps show highways, railroads, and settlements plus large industries, such as coal mines, quarries, and cement plants, so it was not hard to glean useful data about how the AM would earn a living and the type of scenery it would traverse.

Need a town name? Check the map for a town or, failing that, a geographical feature, such as a gap or creek name. That's how I came up with Sunrise, Gap Run, (North) Durbin, Glady, Big Springs, Coal Fork, and Low Gap.

Free index maps of each state are available from the U.S. Geological Survey (Box 25286, Federal Center, Denver CO 80225) and at other locations nationwide. Aerial photos of ports and other facilities are available by writing to the U.S.G.S., 507 National Center, Reston VA 22092.

Topographical maps show contour lines of constant elevation. If they're spread widely apart, they depict a gentle slope. If they're bunched together, the land drops off quickly, much as isobars jammed together on a weather map show areas of high winds, making it easy to spot ravines and ridges.

Fig. 7-10: The Walthers HO scale Trainline depot kit is generic enough to serve as a standard depot for a freelanced railroad. Just add some railroad-specific details and paint it company colors (here for the author's Ridgeley & Midland County short line).

Fig. 7-11: Bill Darnaby got to do some prototype modeling by superimposing the Maumee on an existing junction of two New York Central lines in Edison, Ohio, and featuring the NYC tower.

Cuts, fills, and other artificial terrain alterations are revealed by straight or smoothly curving contour lines. This makes it easier to locate the right-of-way and gather information about the territory traversed by a railroad that was abandoned decades ago (fig. 7-14).

Mountain railroading

When spectacular scenery is a primary goal, it's hard to resist the allure of mountain railroading. I've seen many model railroads that feature stunning mountain vistas gathering a patina of dust due to inactivity, however. A single-track main line

Fig. 7-12: A disadvantage of a multi-level design is that the vertical clearance over the lower deck is limited. Here sight-line restrictions caused by the 13″ of clearance below the fluorescent fixtures cut off the top of the concrete elevator.

winding around craggy peaks with few towns and industries at lineside offers little operating potential. Since the thrill of running trains for their own sake may quickly wane, a mountain railroad needs to integrate scenic grandeur with features that support interesting and realistic operation.

Mountain railroads have to follow natural drainage courses through the peaks, so there are few crossing lines or interchanges. That's a lot to give up (see chapter 8), but all is not lost. A few busy coal mines, as on the Denver & Rio Grande Western (later Southern Pacific and now Union Pacific) around

Helper, Utah, and on most Appalachian coal roads, can generate enough traffic to keep a lot of mine shifter and road crews busy.

The operating potential picks up when you add in crews and the time required to remove helpers ahead of the caboose (see fig. 7-15 and *Realistic Model Railroad*

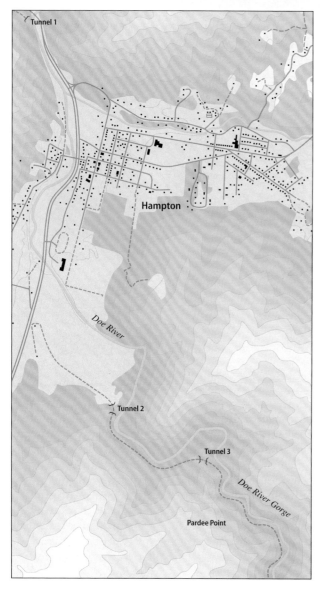

Fig. 7-13: This "test" scene on the author's new HO railroad, shot in about the same location seen in fig. 7-12, shows how a commercial photo mural adds depth to a shallow shelf scene. Having the barn in the backdrop photo shot from one corner instead of "flat-on" minimizes perspective problems when viewing or reshooting the scene. Evenly lighting the scene with photofloods was not a problem despite the overhead upper deck.

Tunnel 1

Hampton

Doe River

Tunnel 2

Tunnel 3

Doe River Gorge

Pardee Point

Fig. 7-14: Comparing the (re-created) U.S. Geological Survey topographic map to the photo of a tourist train at Pardee Point (left) in Doe River Gorge on the former East Tennessee & Western North Carolina shows how contour lines bunch together to indicate steep terrain. The area around Hampton, Tennessee, is relatively flat, so the contour lines are spaced far apart. Tunnels 1 (north of Hampton), 2, and 3 (in the gorge) are shown on the map and help to locate the abandoned right-of-way.

Fig. 7-15: Mountain railroads may lack frequent interchanges, but they compensate with great scenery and pusher operations. Here an articulated helps a heavy eastbound coal drag out of Hinton, West Virginia, on Dan Zugelter's HO scale C&O railroad.

Operation, page 19). Some railroads, even some states, prohibited pushing against wood cabooses or even an occupied caboose for fear it would be crushed or popped off the track like a slice of bread out of a toaster.

This requirement benefits model railroad operation, as it requires an upbound train to drop its caboose behind a crossover or helper spur and pull ahead far enough for the pusher engine(s) to slide into the slot, grab the caboose, and couple to the train. A similar sequence is needed at top of the grade.

Time is distance on a layout. Having "stuff" to do before leaving town or en route adds to the time it takes us to complete a run, and that makes a model railroad seem longer.

Helper grades tend to bunch up trains, as their speed up the mountain is reduced. We need to provide sidings or small yards at the top and bottom of most helper grades to avoid plugging up the railroad. Locating a helper grade just beyond yard limits may prove helpful, as delayed trains have a place to wait off the main. (Yardmasters tend to view this a bit differently, however.)

Railroads that will feature pushers should be planned so that trains need the extra power to climb the hill. Pushing on a train that doesn't need the assistance may cause a derailment, as the pusher will likely bunch the train against the head-end power, possibly popping it off the rails on a curve. The need for pushers can be created by using less powerful head-end power (including dummy units), building more weight into cars, adding heavier loads (such as loose coal in hoppers), running longer trains, and installing trucks that do not roll too freely.

Longer cars are more problematic on mountain railroads, as their ends tend to swing outboard of the rails on tight curves. The projecting coupler acts like a lever that can derail the rear truck of a preceding car. Reverse curves that aren't spaced at least one car-length apart by a length of tangent (straight) track can also cause derailments. Attempting to solve such concerns with free-swinging couplers may cause other problems at other times, like when such cars are pushed during yard switching.

I found that 2.5 percent was a good gradient in combination with the Allegheny Midland's 30″ curves. Most long trains required pushers to get up that grade, and—of equal importance—the grade was not too steep. Locomotive mechanisms may bind up going down steeper grades, causing them to surge, and motors may "cog" as the train tries to make them turn faster. Thrust washers alleviate surging, but avoiding unduly steep grades may be easier.

Overlay all that action with dark territory where timetable and train-order rules apply, and everyone will have his or her head in the game. It's a different style of railroading than that seen in the flatlands, and by making careful choices, railroading in the mountains can offer more than pretty scenery.

Putting the I&StL on the map

In chapter 5, Mike Schafer discusses the creation of a herald for his free-lanced HO scale Illinois & St. Louis Railroad. He wanted to establish a route focusing on Illinois, his home state. The railroad had to serve his two favorite cities, Chicago and St. Louis. Passenger trains have always been Mike's primary interest as a railfan and modeler (he edited *Passenger Train Journal*), and his favorite era is the mid-1960s when he did a lot of railfanning despite his status as "an impoverished high school student."

Mike wanted the I&StL to represent an also-ran carrier, "just your average company that dealt with the day-to-day problems of transportation as best it could during a period of over-regulation and increasing highway competition." Most importantly, he had to have a railroad with a unique asset that would make it successful among a gaggle of competitors between the two cities—a route structure that allowed traffic moving between the East and Southeast and the West to bypass Chicago.

The resulting railroad, as shown in the accompanying map (fig. 7-16), forms a large X, with the Twin Cities at the upper left and Indianapolis at lower right. At the upper right is Chicago linked to St. Louis at lower left. The main lines cross at Peoria, Illinois, another hotbed of railroad activity.

At Minneapolis-St. Paul, the I&StL connects with the Great Northern, Northern Pacific, and Soo Line. The bulk of this traffic is destined for the East and Southeast via Indianapolis, where it has connections with the Pennsylvania, New York Central, and Baltimore & Ohio.

"Even traffic from Milwaukee headed east or to St. Louis can bypass Chicago via Peoria," Mike says. "Traffic for Chicago has an easier route, since the main line from the Twin Cities and Rockford, Illinois, and from St. Louis more or less sidesteps Chicago by swinging around the southwest side of town on its approach to the railroad's yard at Calumet City, Illinois. Here is easy access to the railroad's main ally in moving traffic between east and west, the Erie Lackawanna.

"Some of these traffic patterns apply to passenger service as well," Mike adds. "In 1965, did the nation really need another Chicago–Twin Cities passenger train? Maybe not, but how about a Minneapolis–Peoria–Indianapolis train called the *Mid-American* that connects with the GN's *Empire Builder* and the NP's *North Coast Limited* and takes passengers to St. Louis or Indianapolis (the *Mid-American* splits at Peoria), where they can make easy transfers to trains south and east without having to mess with Chicago?

"With these basics established, it was only a matter of sitting down with maps of the associated midwestern states and connecting the dots. Often, I went with the heart instead of cold pragmatism, choosing towns and cities I've long been intrigued by or have some ties to (Joliet and Peoria, for example)."

The I&StL may be freelanced, but it's clearly established in the midwestern rail network. Mike even opted to share track with the Gulf, Mobile & Ohio between Joliet and Dwight and the Santa Fe between Joliet and Coal City. This arrangement supports the appearance of GM&O equipment and the ATSF's hi-level *El Capitan*. The railroad also parallels another favorite, the once-electrified Illinois Terminal.

After all this, choosing a name "wasn't as easy as it may seem," Mike recalls. "I wanted 'Chicago' in the name, as it conjures up images of intense railroading. I also wanted to use 'Illinois' to fix the railroad's location. My first attempt at naming the railroad back in the mid-1970s produced Chicago, Illinois Central & Eastern, which provided too much information about my prototype and regional preferences.

"Then I tried various combinations: Chicago, St. Louis & Eastern; Chicago North Central; Illinois, Chicago & Eastern; and Chicago, Illinois & Eastern. I finally bit the bullet by dropping 'Chicago' to produce Illinois & St. Louis, which is short and to the point and rolls off the tongue, especially when spoken in reporting-marks form: I-and-Saint-L. It also sounds like the name of a middle-of-the-road company.

"In 1988, the I&StL theme was developed into a 750-square-foot 'test' layout that proved popular with knowledgeable friends despite cramped aisles. Its last run was in the fall of 1997 prior to a move from Wisconsin to Illinois. I built a new house with a larger basement and began work on 'I&StL—The Sequel,' a 1,600-square-foot, bi-level layout that will soon host its first operating session. The layout has changed, but the basic concepts have endured."

CHAPTER EIGHT

Layout design: the visible parts . . .

Layout design can be divided into two key areas: the visible, scenicked portion

of a railroad, and the hidden sections that support that which we see. In this

chapter, I'll look at a number of factors that influence the design of the

scenicked elements. In chapter 9, I'll examine the roles of several

of the key supporting players—staging and fiddle yards.

Fig. 8-1: A mine shifter crew has used its knowledge of the timetable schedule to clear the switch at Run Junction, West Virginia, in time to let a miners train roll by unimpeded on the author's AM. Track plans should be tailored to support the desired type of operation.

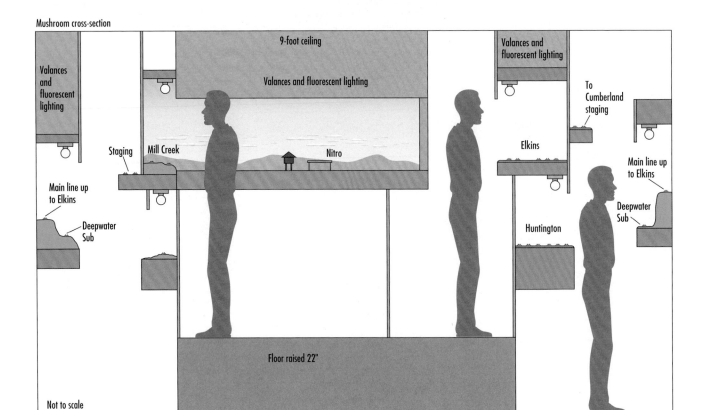

Mushroom cross-section

Valances and fluorescent lighting

9-foot ceiling

Valances and fluorescent lighting

Valances and fluorescent lighting

To Cumberland staging

Main line up to Elkins

Staging

Mill Creek

Nitro

Elkins

Main line up to Elkins

Deepwater Sub

Huntington

Deepwater Sub

Floor raised 22"

Not to scale

The long view

The term "model railroading" comprises both the concept of building models as well as using them in a manner that replicates the purposes of their prototypes. Your knowledge of and interest in operation may be limited today, but putting your models through their paces in a realistic manner is likely to become more important as your knowledge of railroading increases (fig. 8-1). Moreover, there is little cost associated with track planning for realistic operation—unless you build a model railroad now that can't grow with you, leading to its premature demise.

Helping you avoid such pitfalls is an important objective of this chapter and, indeed, the entire book. You may choose to stop anywhere along the path toward greater visual and operational realism, but doing so short of realistic operation denies you the opportunity to learn

about and enjoy a significant part of the hobby's potential.

An operational focus

"Realistic operation" means using our models in a manner that complements their realistic appearance. Think of it as a bonus: You've already gone to the trouble to buy, detail, and/or build a great deal of realism into each model. Sooner or later you may want to enhance that value by using the models in a way that reflects how a full-size railroad goes about business.

Although operations can be added to most model railroads at any time, it's easier to design in key features from the outset. In this chapter, I'll discuss factors of layout design with realistic operation in mind. I'll also review the use of "Layout Design Elements," a concept I introduced in the 1995 issue of *Model Railroad Planning*. Using these ideas can help assure that your layout will have good

operating potential regardless of your present knowledge.

Applying these lessons to an existing railroad may require new construction. You may need to add or expand staging or fiddle yards, cut in crossovers to create runaround tracks, add a passing siding or two so trains can meet at regular intervals along the main line, or reconsider the industries your railroad will serve.

These, however, are the types of ongoing improvements you should constantly be making throughout the life of your railroad. To learn more about realistic operation, please refer to my companion book, *Realistic Model Railroad Operation*.

Layout Design Elements

Few modelers have enough operating knowledge to understand all the subtleties of prototype trackwork arrangements and operating practices. We take our best shot at designing the

Fig. 8-2: As shown by this cross-section of Jerry Bellina's West Virginia Western, a mushroom design precludes operators from seeing trains on more than one level at a time.

trackwork for, say, a small town, only to be disappointed when we find that it isn't much fun to switch or doesn't look quite right. Wouldn't it be easier to selectively compress a suitable prototype town, engine terminal, yard, industry, or key scene to fit our available space?

That's the idea behind using Layout Design Elements: Select interesting prototype sites, like towns, industries, yards, and engine terminals, from one or more railroads of the desired scope, region, and era, and design your layout by arranging them as desired to create your own new railroad. (fig. 8-11). Look to the prototype for layout-design ideas, and follow prototype

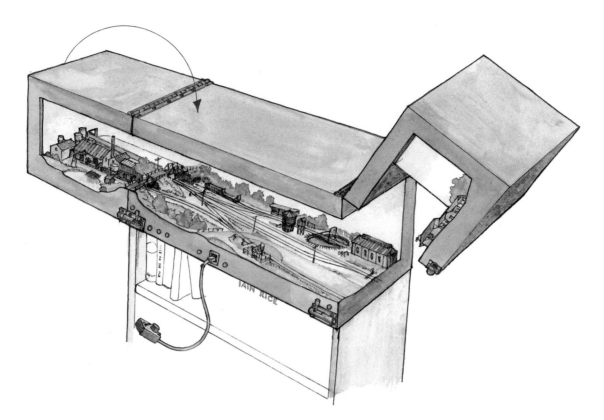

track arrangements as closely as possible, even if you're freelancing.

A major bonus of using Layout Design Elements is that you can proceed with layout design and construction even before you fully understand how a town, yard, engine terminal, or industry works. A full-size railroad used or uses it, so you can assume that it will work. Avoid copying someone else's freelanced track plan, as you have no way to judge whether it worked as well as its designer hoped. Let the prototype be your guide.

Start with a list of key features needed to support the type of railroad you want and select Layout Design Elements accordingly. Choose towns with a variety of passing-track lengths to keep operation interesting. Also, select towns offering the right amount of work for local and through-freight crews to be kept busy but not overwhelmed.

Layout Design Elements are easy to use. First, make to-scale sketches of several towns, a yard or two, and key "signature" scenes on graph paper. Mount them on cardstock and cut them out. Also draw to-scale "puzzle pieces" of staging or fiddle yards. To avoid cheating on the connecting curves, draw several circles of your minimum radius. This will also help you locate turn-back curves or a spiral helix if needed.

Move each Layout Design Element around on a same-scale drawing of the available layout space until most or all of them seem to fit in the proper sequence with sufficient distances between them. You'll quickly discover what will fit and what won't.

Time equals distance

Before you design your model railroad, you need to know what the line is supposed to do and how it is supposed to do it. A small Appalachian coal railroad

set in the 1920s, for example, may boast a fleet of Consolidations (2-8-0s) that will plod around twists and turns and up and down steep grades. A larger coal road would more likely use heavy Mikados (2-8-2s), Mountains (4-8-2s), or articulated compound Mallet (pronounced "Malley") locomotives, such as 2-6-6-2s or 2-8-8-2s.

An advantage of such a slow-paced railroad is that you can locate towns closer together because it will take trains longer to travel between them at 10 scale mph or so. By contrast, a midwestern railroad set in the 1940s or '50s that faced stiff competition from its peers may own fleets of high-drivered 2-8-4s, 4-8-2s, or 4-8-4s that gobble up the distance between towns. That requires a plan that includes mainline runs of approximately 8 to 10 scale miles (500 to 600 actual feet in HO).

Fig. 8-3: With some creativity, you can put a surprising amount of model railroad atop a 1- x 3-foot bookcase. Here Iain Rice suggests using folding wings to stretch the scene.

Scope

If you plan to model the Union Pacific's main line through Nebraska or Wyoming, your first objective will be to find sufficient space to achieve that goal. That may lead you to embrace a multi-level plan, change to a smaller scale, or model an era when the typical freight car was shorter than it is today. Or you may decide such a project is beyond your means and model a branch or short line instead.

But it's just as easy to fall into a trap of another kind when you consider modeling a short or narrow-gauge line that reeks of nostalgia. Regardless of the visual attributes of a railroad's equipment and physical

Fig. 8-4: One of Dan Zugelter's primary objectives was to run long heavyweight C&O passenger trains along the New River. That aim had a major effect on the design of his HO railroad and the era it depicts.

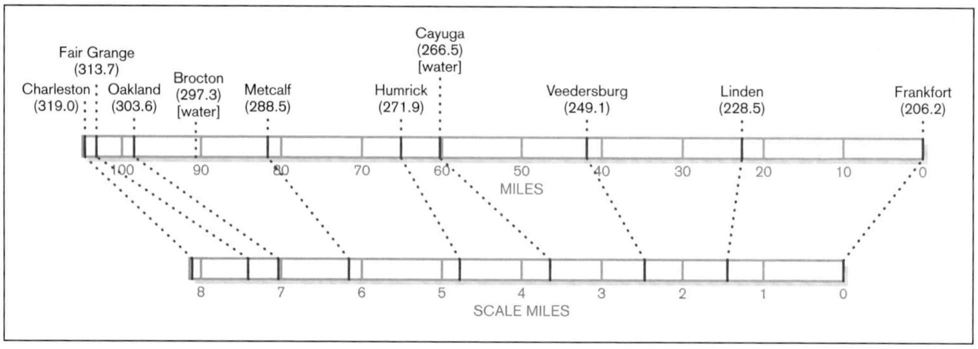

Fair Grange
(313.7)
Charleston : Oakland   Brocton   Metcalf
(319.0) : (303.6)   (297.3)   (288.5)
[water]

Cayuga
(266.5)
[water]
Humrick
(271.9)

Veedersburg
(249.1)

Linden
(228.5)

Frankfort
(206.2)

100   90   80   70   60   50   40   30   20   10   0
MILES

8   7   6   5   4   3   2   1   0
SCALE MILES

Fig. 8-5: This to-scale graph shows towns along the NKP's Third Sub and, below that, the parts the author chose to model. The only modeled water stop at Cayuga (the other was in unmodeled Brocton) was located about midway along the HO main line.

plant, you need to look further down the road toward the day when you'll be doing more operating than building. Will the railroad offer enough challenges and variety to maintain your interest?

The era you choose to model may have a huge bearing on your decision. Many narrow-gauge lines, for example, have attracted large followings due to equipment and environs that beg to be modeled. Yet many of them operated but a single train per day, especially toward the end of their careers. This might satisfy a lone-wolf operator, but it won't support a crew of several modelers.

The bottom line when choosing a prototype to model or use as the basis for freelancing is whether it will be fun to operate when the majority of the modeling challenges are behind you. If not, you're going to tire

of the railroad, and it will either accumulate dust or be relegated to the scrap heap.

Transportation system

Allen McClelland is a pioneer in helping us understand that our model railroads can be seen as integral parts of a transportation system extending "beyond the basement." Fast symbol freights hustle bridge traffic from one division point to the next. Through freights may do some work along the line, especially at busy interchanges to keep hot cars moving toward customers.

The local can now be seen in proper context: It's a means of gathering and distributing cars at industries along the main or on a branch, thus allowing through freights to avoid frequent stops. Cars picked up by through freights and locals are later switched into blocks, and the blocks into

fast or through freights at division-point yards.

Allen's approach to layout design requires staging or fiddle yards at both ends of the main line to simulate through traffic. Long-time students of his Virginian & Ohio will recall how he expanded the original staging yards as his understanding of the potential of staging grew.

Dispatching choices

The way a railroad will be dispatched has a major influence on its design, especially the spacing of passing tracks. A flatlands railroad featuring high-speed operation under timetable and train-order (TT&TO) rules will need enough space between towns to give dispatchers, operators, and crews time to prepare, distribute, read, and react to written instructions. Moreover, the railroad will need several passing tracks to add flexibility to train

movements. Not all passing tracks need be long enough to accommodate the longest trains, adding to the challenge of choosing meet locations.

By modeling a railroad that operates at a slower pace, relatively compact layouts can still support enjoyable TT&TO operation. The operating style will also help determine fast-clock ratios.

Paul Dolkos, whose medium-sized HO scale Boston & Maine features TT&TO operation, observed that clock speeds "should permit enough time for operators to accomplish operating moves without being rushed. I use a 2:1 ratio, and when I revised my timetable I set the passenger schedules so that operators had enough time to make the required engine changes and car adds and drops. If I felt they could do this in 15 actual minutes, then

Fig. 8-6: An interchange can take many forms, such as a leg of a wye at a grade crossing or a siding where a short line terminates at a trunk line. This photo and plan show the Pennsylvania Railroad-Maumee crossing at Sciotovale, Ohio. The interchange track is at the left. The PRR local comes out of a hidden staging track, works the interchange, turns on the wye, and heads back to the staging.

I allowed 30 fast-time minutes on the schedule."

If you're planning a Centralized Traffic Control system (fig. 11-4), then train movement instructions can be issued in seconds by moving a few levers and pushing a button. This lets you space passing tracks closer together, since it's the dispatcher, not train crews, who is making the train movement decisions. Whether a crew can see that the way to the next town is clear doesn't matter; they must obey signal indications.

This situation illustrates a downside to CTC on a model railroad: Train crews have no "skin in the game." They can leave the thinking to the dispatcher, who calls all the shots. As crews wait for signals to clear before proceeding, extraneous conversations with other operators may ensue, distracting everyone and reducing the quality of the session. That's one reason why timetable and train-order operation, in which crews make the go or stay decisions, is gaining in popularity.

Of course, any dispatching system will work as long as it's employed correctly. The key is matching the railroad's design to the type of system being considered.

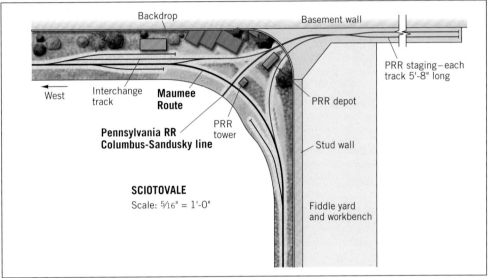

Backdrop

Basement wall

West ←

Interchange track

Maumee Route

Pennsylvania RR Columbus-Sandusky line

PRR tower

PRR depot

Stud wall

SCIOTOVALE
Scale: 5/16" = 1'-0"

PRR staging–each track 5'-8" long

Fiddle yard and workbench

Layout size

If you're pondering how much railroad you can build, maintain, and operate, you'll want to read Paul Dolkos' essay in the 2004 issue of *Model Railroad Planning*. Some of the concerns are obvious: How much time, money, space, and experience do you have? Is model railroading important enough for you to budget time and funds for the layout?

For a number of modelers, the process of selecting or building what they deem to be a suitable site for their layout hinges on criteria related to layout design. I exasperated several real estate agents as they tried to find a suitable basement under an existing house before we decided to build our current home. They were thinking 4 x 8 plywood in a rec room; I was thinking Appalachian empire in a full basement.

But I overlooked something: I could have had the builder add another course or two of blocks to the foundation at little added cost, thus making the basement suitable for a mushroom-style plan, which requires lots of headroom (fig. 8-2).

Still, not everyone has the luxury of a basement or house. If you're having a tough time finding space for even a modest layout, I recommend that you review the many track plans designed to fit atop a small

bookcase that were featured in *Model Railroad Planning* 2003. Two are reprinted here (figs. 8-3 and 8-11).

As *MRP*'s editor, my goal was to show modelers that there is space for a layout or section thereof if they're creative. Other small plans were featured in Iain Rice's books, *Small, Smart & Practical Track Plans* (Kalmbach, 2000) and *Mid-sized & Manageable Track Plans* (Kalmbach, 2003).

Conversely, those of you with lots of space can rest assured that you can build and maintain a large home layout if you build it well from the outset (see chapter 10). You'll probably get discouraged from time to time as roadblocks appear,

Fig. 8-7: The author's ill-advised attempt to separate Sunrise Yard from SN Cabin resulted in a view-blocking ridge (left). It later came out, but the bridge survived to separate the scene into two "events" (above).

funds or available time come up short, and family matters arise, but over the long haul you can get there.

Point-to-point versus continuous run

Unless you're modeling a very short line, your model railroad will depict only a small part of a full-size railroad. Nevertheless, even that segment will run from one point to another. It may, for example, represent a single town, as on many British exhibition layouts. Trains can run into it from a hidden staging or fiddle area and then go back into hiding again. That's called an out-and-return plan, a variation of point-to-point operation. No continuous operation is possible or desired with such an arrangement.

A railroad that runs between two non-connected end points is a true point-to-point plan. Some plans feature end connections that allow the layout to be operated as a continuous loop for demonstration or locomotive break-in purposes, yet operated as a

point-to-point railroad by ignoring the continuous-run connection during operating sessions. Dan Zugelter's Chesapeake & Ohio (figs. 2-1, 7-15, and 8-4) layout is operated point-to-point but has a through staging yard.

Dan's approach enables him to run trains continuously for guests yet still run eastbound loaded coal trains as needed by having them appear out of hidden staging, run over the railroad, re-enter staging, and wait there until needed as another coal train later in the day. Empties are routed westbound in a similar manner, thus keeping loads headed east and empties west, as they should be. Fly-over loops allow passenger trains to return back the way they came, thus keeping Pacifics on the gentle riverside grades and allowing heavier Mountains to repeatedly tackle the climb to the summit at the West Virginia-Virginia line.

The traditional toy-train layout is an oval, figure-eight, dog-bone, or other shape

that allows continuous running. Such layouts tend to be small, so making a single lap isn't much of a run. Some enterprising scale modelers have adapted continuous-run plans to more realistic operation by specifying a set number of laps between towns.

The idea is that there is nothing any more arbitrary about such operations than if cars are randomly moved between towns and industries. There is a business plan for each and every car and train movement.

Track plan schematics

John Armstrong urged drawing a straight-line schematic of a proposed track plan as insurance against surprises. It's a good idea to start with a schematic plan of the prototype or, if freelancing, key parts of the base prototype(s). Mark on it important features, such as water tanks, coal docks, branch-line junctions, interchanges with other railroads, key industries, major scenic features, and

other "givens and druthers," as John liked to put it— things you must have and things you'd like to have.

A schematic map of the NKP's Third Sub of its St. Louis Division (fig. 8-5) shows towns and cities on the prototype. The other schematic shows which ones I picked as Layout Design Elements to model. Both schematics are to scale; that is, towns are located at proportional distances along the line according to their milepost. This offers insights about locations for model towns.

For a steam-era layout, for example, it wouldn't do to locate the one town I plan to model that had a water tank (Cayuga, Indiana) close to either division point. If I had selected Cayuga as the first town west of Frankfort to be modeled, then I might have opted to also model Brocton, Illinois, to balance water tank locations on the layout. But I'm modeling 1954, when Brocton no longer had an interchange with another railroad. Therefore, it's a poor candidate to model from an operational standpoint. Since Cayuga's water tank sits somewhere near the middle of the modeled main line, that wasn't a concern.

Interchanges

The ability to interchange cars and even entire trains

between railroads is perhaps the most important aspect of the rail network. A primary consideration when selecting towns to model is whether or not that town had an interchange. This criterion can't be observed on most mountain railroads, which tend to follow narrow river valleys and have end-to-end connections with foreign railroads rather than at-grade crossings, but there are exceptions.

In the flatlands, rail lines form a grid that looks like a net. Where they cross at grade, there is usually an interchange track or two (fig. 8-6) to allow cars from one line to be spotted for pick up by the other. This track is typically one leg of a wye in a quadrant of the crossing, although two legs may be used so each railroad has a specific setout or pickup track.

Even if a model railroad located in the agriculture belt had no switching opportunities other than interchanges, several local and road crews could still keep busy during a run over a division. Also, car types would be quite varied.

I call interchange tracks "universal industries" because you can find almost any type and quantity of freight car on them. You don't even have to build a structure to model an interchange! (Structure modelers, take heart: Depots, towers, grain elevators, lumberyards, and coal or fuel dealers were seldom far from most interchange points.)

Better yet, interchanges typically operate "under the gun." That is, the clock may be a critical part of an interchange's function because time-critical cars can be switched from one railroad for immediate pickup by the connecting line. That's why interchanges are often switched by through freights instead of plodding peddlers.

A good example of such an interchange was the Nickel Plate Road-Monon interchange at Linden, Indiana (fig. 8-14). The Monon learned through experience that it could

depend on the NKP to make time-critical connections with, for example, auto-parts cars to and from the Ford plant in Louisville, Kentucky. The NKP didn't even run an eastbound local on this part of its St. Louis Division; eastbound through freights stopped there to set out or pick up interchanged traffic to the tune of 12,000 loads swapped annually between the two railroads.

Interchanges can be active or passive. An active interchange is fed by a hidden staging track long enough to accommodate one or more locomotives and the cars of the foreign railroad. Alternatively, fresh cuts of newly arriving cars for interchange could be supplied by a hidden pusher engine or a ramp steep enough to cause more cars to roll into view as preceding cuts are picked up. A passive interchange is a stub track long enough to accommodate the day's traffic.

"Events" versus train length

There are many ways to increase the apparent

Fig. 8-8: Before building any benchwork, the author redrew the AM track plan on kraft paper. After making adjustments, he erected benchwork and checked the plan for reach-in distances and viewing problems before cutting roadbed.

distances between scenes and towns on our model railroads. A key one is what I call "events." If a train runs through a scene in full view, that's one event. If it goes under a bridge about midway through that same scene, that's three events; traversing one part of the scene, going out of sight under the bridge, and continuing through the scene. The total run is thus more visually interesting.

Most scenes can be subdivided into two or three events. Instead of a bridge, you might insert a short tunnel or have a train go into a cut or behind a tall structure or a tree or two placed between the aisle and the main line.

Be sure the event-creating scenery or structure isn't in

73

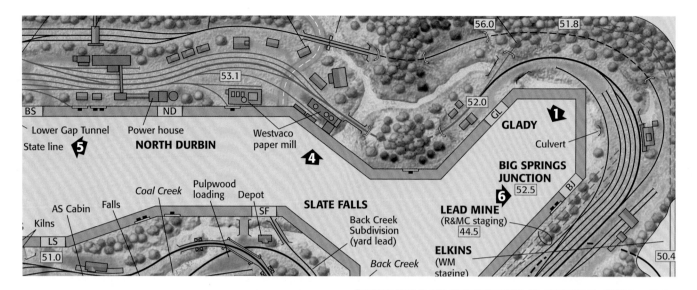

BS | ND
Lower Gap Tunnel | Power house
State line **5**
NORTH DURBIN
53.1
Westvaco paper mill
56.0 | 51.8
52.0
GL
4
GLADY
Culvert
1
BIG SPRINGS JUNCTION
52.5
BJ
AS Cabin | Falls | *Coal Creek* | Pulpwood loading | Depot
Kilns
LS
51.0
SF
SLATE FALLS
Back Creek Subdivision (yard lead)
LEAD MINE (R&MC staging)
44.5
6
ELKINS (WM staging)
Back Creek
50.4

the way when it comes time to switch cars. I inserted part of a ridge near the yard throat at Sunrise, Virginia, on the Allegheny Midland to visually separate the yard from a nearby junction, and it got in the yardmaster's way. I removed the ridge but retained a road bridge (fig. 8-7), thus subdividing the main scene without handicapping the yardmaster.

Train length can also be partially determined by the use of scene dividers. If viewers cannot readily see both ends of a train from any vantage point, trains can be shorter than on layouts where it's easy to see the entire train at a glance. There are limits to such sleights-of-hand—my original plans to run trains of 12 to 15 cars on the AM proved shortsighted, and I had to lengthen the major passing tracks to accommodate trains of 25 cars or longer.

I designed my new NKP layout with 18-foot passing tracks to accommodate trains with approximately 30 cars. Even then, however, where trains pass behind an elevator or interlocking tower or duck under an overhead road bridge, they seem longer than trains racing down a mile-long tangent.

A 25-car train in HO

Fig. 8-9: This part of the AM track plan shows how the benchwork "lobe" (projection) to the left (south) of Glady made it difficult for crews working there or at Big Springs Junction to see how close the next town (North Durbin) was.

Fig. 8-10: Usurping the storage end of the garage—and a little more (the car noses under the benchwork) —increased the length of the main line by 30 feet per level, or a scale mile overall!

looks longer than a 25-car train in N. Modelers using a track plan drawn for a larger scale than the one they're working in would do well to allow for longer passing and yard tracks instead of scaling down the original plan. Similarly, reducing an HO plan with 30″ curves to N with 16″ curves results in curves that appear too sharp. It's good practice, therefore, to draw planned curves on kraft paper, put rolling stock on them (fig. 8-8), and view them at the planned height to see if they look right.

Lobes

Anything that interferes with sight lines between sections of a layout will help disguise its relatively compact

size. A technique I used on the AM is a benchwork bulge I call a "lobe." A lobe is nothing more than a mini-peninsula that juts 1 to 3 feet into an aisle, thus blocking a viewer's eye. Used in conjunction with curves, lobes help disguise the short distances between towns.

Figure 8-9 shows a lobe at

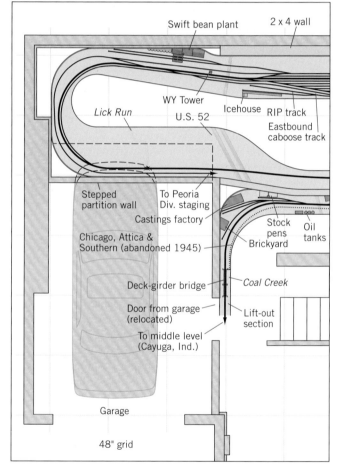

Swift bean plant | 2 x 4 wall
Lick Run
WY Tower
U.S. 52
Icehouse | RIP track
Eastbound caboose track
Stepped partition wall
To Peoria Div. staging
Castings factory
Chicago, Attica & Southern (abandoned 1945)
Stock pens
Brickyard
Oil tanks
Deck-girder bridge
Coal Creek
Door from garage (relocated)
To middle level (Cayuga, Ind.)
Lift-out section
Garage
48″ grid

Glady between Big Springs Junction and North Durbin, West Virginia, where the Allegheny Midland main line joined the Western Maryland's Elkins line. Imagine yourself running a southbound train (to the left) through Big Springs Junction. Glady is just behind you, but you don't

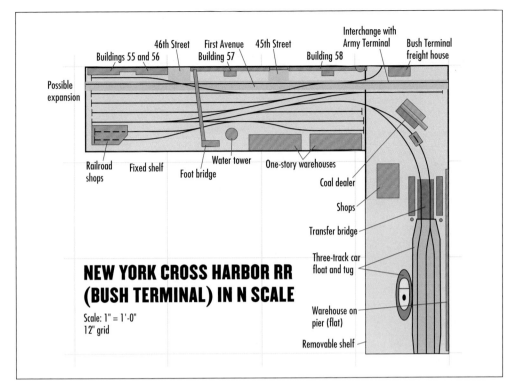

Buildings 55 and 56 · 46th Street · First Avenue Building 57 · 45th Street · Building 58 · Interchange with Army Terminal · Bush Terminal freight house

Possible expansion

Railroad shops · Fixed shelf · Foot bridge · Water tower · One-story warehouses · Coal dealer · Shops · Transfer bridge · Three-track car float and tug · Warehouse on pier (flat) · Removable shelf

NEW YORK CROSS HARBOR RR (BUSH TERMINAL) IN N SCALE

Scale: 1" = 1'-0"
12" grid

Fig. 8-11: Bernie Kempinski's bookcase-top plan plus an extension featuring the New York Cross Harbor (see fig. 7-8) is an example of a Layout Design Element. Following the prototype example helps ensure that the model will be equally interesting to scenic and operate.

notice that because you're facing away from it.

As you follow your train southward, you gradually turn to face Glady, but the ridge line on the lobe precludes directly viewing the next town, North Durbin. Big Springs Junction is now behind you. Had the two towns been located along a straight section of benchwork, you could have easily noticed that your train is probably in both sites at the same time.

Garages are for   railroads!

The lobe trick wouldn't work on the flatlands NKP. To increase the distance between towns, I added a second level to the railroad, which doubled the mainline run. At Frank Hodina's suggestion, I extended one aisle into the back of the garage (fig. 8-10). This required building a new knee wall with the "jog" high enough to clear the first foot or so of the hood of an automobile. I insulated the knee wall and covered the exterior side with ⅝"–thick

wallboard to meet fire codes.

The garage is only 13 feet wide, so why go to so much trouble? The gain is substantial, as a train entering the former garage area travels about 15 feet by the time it's halfway around the turn-back curve and then goes another 15 feet back into the original basement area. It does that twice, once on the lower deck and once on the upper, during its run between division-point yards. That's 60 feet total, or one scale mile in HO! Since the entire main line is only about 8 scale miles long, including the two garage excursions, that's a huge gain.

Prototype interaction

If you're freelancing, you'll need all the help you can get to convince viewers that your railroad is a part of the continental transportation network. Jim Paine's freelanced Durham & Southern interchanged with Allen McClelland's V&O and the Norfolk & Western. The latter located the D&S in time and place.

However, Allen originally interchanged only with other freelanced railroads, as he valued the social aspects of the resulting interplay between friends. The V&O nevertheless came to be regarded as one of the best examples of prototype freelancing. Allen has since begun using pooled power with actual regional railroads, such as the Chesapeake & Ohio and the Seaboard Coast Line, and Amtrak trains now operate over V&O rails, increasing the realism and making the V&O's traffic patterns easier to understand.

Curves and turnouts

The major constraint on most layout designs is not cost or time but space. This directly affects scope, as a closet-shelf layout is unlikely to permit you to build a convincing segment of a busy main line. That said, you could opt to build a single town along a main line and feed it with staging yards off either end. Even a 4- x 8-foot layout can provide a lot

of action if the front half is used for a town and the back half—behind a backdrop— for a staging or fiddle yard.

A continuous-run plan, such as an oval on a 4 x 8, adds an important restriction compared to a linear layout fed by stud-ended staging or fiddle yards: curves. You can't have curves any larger than a 22″ radius on a 48″-wide platform, and even that is pushing it.

Such considerations make an along-the-wall shelf layout much less restrictive than any free-standing platform. You can use a relatively large minimum radius in a corner of a room without unduly impinging on the floor space.

Another consideration is how longer equipment will look on your chosen minimum radius. My Berkshires, Mountains, and 2-6-6-2s could negotiate the AM's 30″ curves, but boilers and cabs exhibited considerable overhang, as did full-length passenger cars.

Bill Darnaby built a series of test curves using flextrack

Fig. 8-12: A 42″-radius curve avoids unrealistically extreme cab and pilot overhang. Spiral easements (transition curves) between straight and curved track also improve a locomotive's appearance as it enters or leaves a curve; furthermore, moderate superelevation contributes to greater realism.

Fig. 8-13: The AM's yards were built at 43″ above the floor—obviously a bit low for realistic viewing (left)—to allow vertical room for a long climb to the 54″ summit. Bill Darnaby switches the Maumee's yard at Dacron, Ohio, which at 66″ provides a realistic "railfan's view" of the railroad.

to find the tightest curve that was still broad enough for his 4-8-2s to look realistic while negotiating them and decided on a 42″ minimum radius. Similar tests with my 2-8-4s produced the same answer (fig. 8-12).

Easements—spiral curves between tangents and true circles—help locomotives enter curves without being abruptly jerked to one side. I draw tangents so they pass by the outside of the circle's arc by about ⅝″ and then bend a wood yardstick into a smooth easement connecting the two segments. Making a cardstock template of a typical easement saves time.

It's a good idea to buy a few sample track components and dummy up a yard ladder on a piece of plywood. Then you can simulate back-and-forth switching moves using your longest locomotives and cars. You may find a no. 4 turnout is troublesome but a no. 5 works fine yet looks too sharp for your tastes. If you plan to operate locomotives with long wheelbases, you may find even a no. 6 is pushing your luck.

Use flextrack to mock up a minimum-radius curve and add one with a radius 2″ larger (in HO) to simulate an adjacent passing track. Will your longest cars and stiffest locomotives negotiate the minimum-radius curve with ease? And will such cars and locomotives cleanly pass? Steam locomotive pilots,

walkways, steps, and cabs often stick out in harm's way. If any elements create problems, move the outer track out from the minimum-radius curve in 1/16″ or 1/8″ increments until you obtain adequate clearance. In addition, use spiral easements between curves and tangents.

Should you need to increase the minimum radius, doing so in all but "one spot in a tight corner" won't work; a minimum is a minimum. The only exception is when you use true operational minimum-radius curves in hidden areas and broader

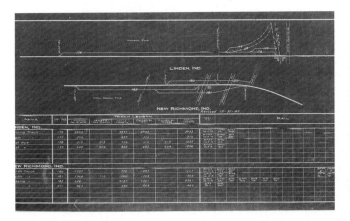

"visual" minimum-radius curves in scenicked areas. The actual minimum is the one that all equipment reliably negotiates.

If you can't achieve the required or desired minimum radius, perhaps you should rethink your roster choices. That could lead you to reconsider your choice of prototype or, if freelancing, base prototype(s). It's better to make the tough decisions up front, as equipment that doesn't operate almost perfectly and look reasonably realistic won't satisfy you over the long haul.

I superelevate (raise the outer rail of) all mainline curves by aligning a continuous strip of 1/16" wood shims under the outer end of the ties. I sand the strip to a feather edge beginning just before the curve, and let it ramp up to full height over a foot or so. This adds considerable realism but isn't enough to cause cars to tip to the inside of the curve.

Turnouts are essentially curves. Most equipment operates through turnouts that look abrupt (fig. 6-12). The only way to choose a minimum turnout frog number—a ratio of the distance from the frog point to where the rails have spread apart one unit—is to test turnouts of various sizes and brands using the equipment you plan to operate.

When drawing your track plan, take care to draw the frog angles accurately with a template. Too often I see overly optimistic plans drawn with no. 2 frogs instead of a more reasonable no. 5 or 6. I used no. 6 frogs on the AM except for crossovers, where I used no. 8s. On the NKP, I'm using no. 8s on the main and in crossovers, and 6s or 7s elsewhere.

Grades

Grades offer similar design challenges. On the AM, I made many tests to see what grades were steep enough to require helpers on trains of typical tonnage, yet not so steep as to cause engines to surge going down them (adding thrust washers to the gearbox usually cures this problem). The data pointed to a 2.5 percent grade, which years of operation confirmed.

The NKP presented a different challenge. The railroad had to climb steadily around the room and along the central peninsula to reach the second deck, yet helpers were not appropriate. Experience with Bill Darnaby's Maumee Route suggested that grades of 1 percent were adequate to separate the two main levels though not so steep as to restrict the length of trains powered by a single Mountain or Berkshire.

I chose to have the grade in the westbound direction. The division's 1.29 percent ruling grade faced just westbounds just west of Cayuga, Indiana, so I've stiffened the gradient there enough to give the engineers on heavy freights a challenge. Like their professional counterparts, they will occasionally have to double the hill: take the first half of the train up to the summit at Humrick, Illinois, and return for the rest of the train.

Multi-level layout design

When I tried to design my new NKP layout, I found that the longest main line I could squeeze in on one level was around 250 feet—far short of the 600-foot main that helps to make the Maumee so rewarding to operate under TT&TO rules. I tried to justify the short mainline run by planning to model only the Indiana half of the Third Sub between the classification yard at Frankfort, Indiana, and a staging yard representing the Illinois half.

Then Bill Darnaby offered an important piece of layout-design logic. Wouldn't it be more realistic and fulfilling if each road engineer had the opportunity to pick up his or her engine on the "pit" by the coal dock or diesel fuel cranes, make a run over the entire division, yard the train, and leave the locomotive on the pit at the next division-point yard? Contrast that with an engineer leaving a

Fig. 8-14: These two NKP track diagrams show that the busiest location at Linden, Indiana, is at the east (right) end of the passing track, whereas the focus at Metcalf, Illinois, is at the west end. These two towns therefore make good "vertical pairs" on a multi-level layout, as crews working in both towns won't get in each other's way.

yard, making a short run, and heading into staging at some point along the division.

Bill's comment caused me to adopt a multi-level design. Where I had previously viewed multi-level layout designs as being too complex and scenically destitute, I now saw this approach to layout design as a golden opportunity. I couldn't serve two masters—scenery and operation—with equal finesse. Since I wanted to re-create NKP operations in the 1950s, operational needs assumed their rightful place at the top of my track-planning priority list.

Experience on other layouts and construction on the Third Sub have confirmed the wisdom of Bill's advice. Even my fear that the space between decks was too confining for realistic photography lighting proved unfounded (fig. 7-13).

Other concerns

Several other concerns surfaced as I was designing

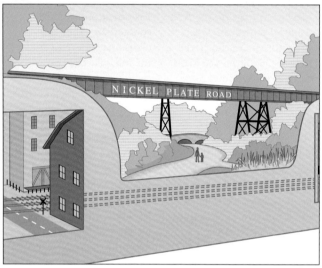

Fig. 8-15: Making an accurate model of this bridge scene depicting the author's father and oldest son is a primary objective, but it's located on the second level above grain elevators in downtown Frankfort. Solution: Use a combined fascia-valance and grain elevator walls to hide the view of the valley.

For more information

Members of the NMRA's Layout Design Special Interest Group (www.ldsig.org) participate in highly informative discussions online and at many regional and national conventions. Their *Layout Design Journal* alone is worth the dues, which include four mailings.

my new layout. First, there is only one ideal level for a layout, and both levels of a two-deck railroad can't be at that height. Odds are, neither one will be at an ideal level (fig. 8-13), so it pays to do a litttle testing first. Gather some cement blocks or gallon paint cans and pieces of heavy cardboard or wood planks and use them to mock-up sections of benchwork at the levels you are considering. Can you see and reach the rear-most tracks on both levels? Do you need to accommodate any unusually tall or short crew or family members?

Multi-level layouts have the potential to almost double aisle congestion, though this is mainly a function of train density. If you run trains on streetcar frequencies, you'll need wider aisles. Wide aisles also make

it easier to view and photograph a layout. Nevertheless, narrow aisle sections here and there are reasonable choices if they allow you to build a longer main line. Just be sure there are wider areas on either side of pinch points where crews can meet and pass.

It's a good idea to offset towns laterally when they are located above and below the other, but this is often impossible. A more practical approach is to choose towns that have the focus of operation at opposite ends. Compare the NKP track diagrams (fig. 8-14) for Linden, Indiana, and Metcalf, Illinois, which is

located directly above Linden. Note that the NKP's busy interchange at Linden with the Monon is on the east (right) end of town, whereas its interchange with the Baltimore & Ohio at Metcalf is at the west (left) end of town. These towns make good "vertical pairs," as crews working the towns at the same time will be as much as 20 feet apart.

You will also discover that putting "deep" scenes, such as a bridge over a river (fig. 8-15), on the upper level is problematic in that they project down into the lower scene. Decks can seldom be spaced more than 18″ apart and are often much closer,

so any dip in upper-level scenery merits study. At the very least, don't locate any busy operating areas directly below such depressions.

You may be able to avoid the need for space-eating helixes on large multi-level layouts by having track climb gradually along the exterior walls and a central peninsula from the lower to the upper level. This technique was used for Bill Darnaby's Maumee (*Model Railroad Planning* 1998) and my Third Subdivision of the NKP's St. Louis line (September and October 2000 *Model Railroader*). Flatlands motive power can negotiate the gradual (1 percent or so) climb with trains of reasonable length (25 to 30 cars), whereas a steep climb up a helix might prohibit such a lengthy train.

CHAPTER NINE
. . . and the invisible parts

In chapter 8, I reviewed design considerations for the scenicked, or visible, part of a layout. What we don't see on a model railroad is equally important, as that is where the stage is set for the sections we model. Operational realism depends, to a great extent, on how we manage the illusion of the railroad's contact with the rest of the continental rail network. This is typically handled with hidden staging or fiddle yards. Be they passive or active, hidden or visible, staging yards provide a way for cars to enter and leave the modeled portion of a railroad. Even a car ferry (fig. 9-1) can act as a form of staging.

Fig. 9-1: A ferry that sails to make connections with the outside world is part of normal operations on Paul Scoles' Sn3 Pelican Bay Railway & Navigation Co. As seen in fig. 9-12, a crew member carries the *G.T. Chrey* to a nearby staging yard, where the cars are replaced. Sn3 (⁹⁄₆₄" to the foot, 1:64) is an ideal size for narrow-gauge layouts.

Fig. 9-2: Staging yards are passive—train consists are not reworked during an operating session—and often hidden. Trackwork must therefore be first rate. The author inserted rerailers every few lengths of track in his new east-end staging yard.

Fig. 9-3: The two photos below show how staging yards can be tucked under scenicked portions of a railroad. Note how the turnouts in the NKP's east-end staging yard ladder (right) are aligned along the aisle to ensure easy access. (Also see fig. 10-4.)

Definitions

A staging yard (fig. 9-2) holds complete trains made up prior to an operating session, then dispatches or accepts them during the actual session. Access isn't usually required during the session. It's "passive" in that cars and trains aren't made up in real time during the session (fig. 9-3).

A fiddle yard (fig. 9-4) is accessible and "active" during a session, allowing operations to continue indefinitely. The concept originated in the United Kingdom to facilitate continuous operation on small, one-town layouts during public exhibitions. An unseen fiddle-yard operator swaps cars or consists to meet a preset train schedule. The goal is to impress and entertain the observer, not the operator.

Staging yards

The utility of railroads is largely due to their being part of a network. Only a handful of full-size railroads, such as utility-owned lines that ran between coal mines and power plants (fig. 3-6), existed in isolation. This fact makes it difficult to design a plausible railroad without including connections with the outside world.

Some connections are made via interchanges, where one railroad crosses or connects end-to-end with another (fig. 8-6). Other important connections may be with the next division or a branch line of a railroad. Even if you're modeling one end of a trunk-line railroad, you'll need to create a way for cars to continue to connecting lines, be they other trunk lines or urban belt lines that shuffle cars between railroads.

This is where staging yards come into play. They allow trains to seemingly come from or go to places beyond the modeled portion of your railroad. Trains placed there before the "day" begins come onto the railroad sequentially as needed or as a schedule requires. Trains headed for distant locales or consists built during the day will head into such yards, thus seeming to continue their runs beyond the confines of the scenicked layout.

You can save space by eliminating classification yards. Instead, build the scenicked "twisty bits" between division-point yards and allow all the car-sorting and -forwarding functions normally performed by the classification yard to be handled either by the staging yard, typically between operating sessions, or by the fiddle yard in real time.

The no-visible-yards approach, though feasible, won't be favored by those who enjoy the challenges of keeping a classification yard fluid or seeing a changing parade of freight cars. It also precludes engine crews from enjoying the sense of accomplishment that comes from making a complete run over a division, however truncated it may be.

The easiest way to add

Fig. 9-4: Jack Ozanich took these two photos of the fiddle yard on his Atlantic Great Eastern. It's designed like a normal classification yard but isn't fully scenicked. Storage shelves make it easy to change consists, and a turntable precludes picking up locomotives to turn them.

staging to a railroad is to build a handful of stub-ended storage tracks at one or both ends of the main line (fig. 9-2). They take little space and can often be located along a wall in an adjacent room, behind a water heater, over a workbench, on a bookshelf, under the benchwork (fig. 9-3), or over the scenicked part of the railroad. You can use a sector plate (fig. 9-5) to switch trains onto yard or staging tracks without resorting to a space-consuming turn-back curve.

A potential problem with "muzzle-loading" (stub-ended) staging yards is that you can't reuse trains after they enter such yards during the session. The session is

over when all staged trains have been run, and trains must be restaged before the next session. Train consists must be reblocked and cabooses and engines have to be moved to the opposite ends of each train.

But the railroad may not need to be restaged after every session. If you use a 6:1 clock and a session lasts 4 actual hours, you have to restage the railroad after each operating session. If you use a 3:1 clock and run only half the day's schedule during each 4-hour session, you have to restage the railroad after every other session. Use a 2:1 clock with each session representing an 8-hour "trick" and you only have to restage every third session, assuming there's enough

traffic to keep your crew busy for 4 actual hours.

If you run lots of look-alike coal drags or commuter trains, then a loop-type staging yard will allow you to reuse equipment during the session. A loop staging yard has a larger footprint than a stub-ended yard with an equal number of tracks, so locating it in the same area as a "blob" (John Armstrong's colorful term for a turn-back curve) at the end of a peninsula or in a helix will save considerable floor space.

Each loop track requires two turnouts and the associated controls, and there are also twice as many fouling points. Moreover, the yard constitutes a reversing loop, which creates the potential for short circuits

if crews are not adept at operating the electrical controls, although automatic reversing circuits have virtually eliminated such concerns for those using Digital Command Control.

Byron Henderson devised a clever X-shaped arrangement of two stub-ended staging yards that allows trains to run from one modeled scene into staging, back unseen through a hidden connection into the other staging yard, and reappear in the other modeled scene (fig. 9-6). He describes what he dubbed "X-factor staging" in the 2004 edition of *Model Railroad Planning*.

Mike Hamer located a "surround-staging" yard around the perimeter of

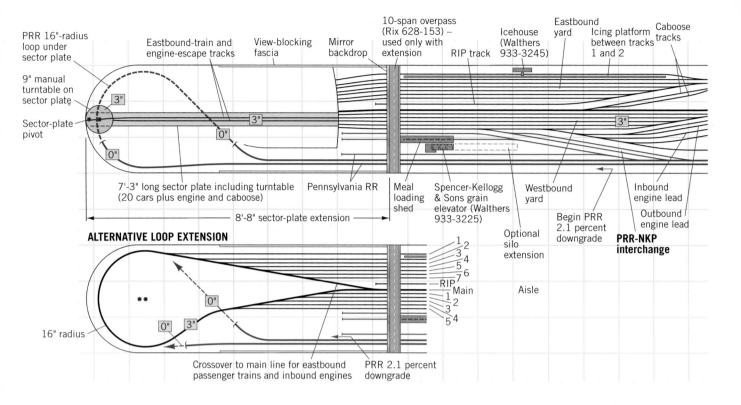

PRR 16"-radius loop under sector plate

9" manual turntable on sector plate

Sector-plate pivot

Eastbound-train and engine-escape tracks

View-blocking fascia

Mirror backdrop

10-span overpass (Rix 628-153) – used only with extension

RIP track

Icehouse (Walthers 933-3245)

Eastbound yard

Icing platform between tracks 1 and 2

Caboose tracks

3"

3"

0"

3"

0"

7'-3" long sector plate including turntable (20 cars plus engine and caboose)

Pennsylvania RR

Meal loading shed

Spencer-Kellogg & Sons grain elevator (Walthers 933-3225)

Westbound yard

Inbound engine lead

8'-8" sector-plate extension

Optional silo extension

Begin PRR 2.1 percent downgrade

Outbound engine lead

PRR-NKP interchange

ALTERNATIVE LOOP EXTENSION

0"

0"

3"

16" radius

1 2
3 4
5 6
7
RIP
1 2
3
5 4

Main

Aisle

Crossover to main line for eastbound passenger trains and inbound engines

PRR 2.1 percent downgrade

Fig. 9-5: A sector plate pivots at one end to allow it to be aligned with other visible or hidden tracks. This one is a full N scale train-length long and includes two tracks and a turntable to allow eastbound steam locomotives to be turned and run around to the other end of their trains to create westbounds.

his railroad room behind a low sky backdrop. He explains this flexible and space-saving idea in *MRP* 2001 and *Realistic Model Railroad Operation.*

Determining staging needs

When planning a stub-ended staging yard, you must first determine the maximum number of trains (including extras, sections, and specials) in both directions that will operate over the railroad during a typical operating session. That gives a rough approximation of the number of staging tracks required.

Be aware, however, that operating six eastbound and six westbound trains doesn't

mean that you need only six staging tracks at each end of the railroad. If one or more eastbounds leave the west-end staging yard before any westbounds depart, there won't be any place for them to go.

Paul Faulk therefore put his schedule on a spreadsheet so he could see the effects of schedule requirements and changes on train movements and hence staging track needs, as he described in the 1997 issue of *Model Railroad Planning.*

Fiddle yards

Fiddle yards (fig. 9-4) are, by definition, hidden from ready view. The idea is that even a small exhibition layout can seem to operate an endless number of freight and passenger trains, thanks to a member of the crew who works behind the scenes to switch or remove "used" trains and put new ones on the rails.

These yards allow layouts to operate indefinitely, since trains are continuously being

renewed in real time. If the fiddle yard is designed to look and function much like a normal classification yard, it offers enough action and challenge to attract crewmembers that find yard work stimulating.

Fiddle yards generate a greater variety of trains and equipment than any type of staging yard, and they support operating sessions of any length. The realism of the railroading experienced by the "mole" doing the fiddling is somewhat diminished, but everyone else's experience is enhanced by the limitless number and variety of operating trains.

Visible staging

While we're on the topic of staging, let's shift our focus back to the visible part of the railroad. Not all staging yards need to be hidden from view. David Barrow prefers visible staging yards (see *Realistic Model Railroad Operation*, page 37). His approach works well for relatively modern railroads,

where it is not unusual to see several trains being held out of a classification yard.

This is not appropriate for the steam era, however, as steam locomotives cannot be left unattended for long periods. I therefore employ hidden staging yards for my railroad, which is set in 1954. Tucking the east-end staging yard two levels below a division-point yard and the west-end staging above a rural bridge scene also saved floor space.

The downside of below-deck hidden staging becomes apparent when a train on an inner track derails and intervening trains must be moved out of the way to allow the errant cars to be reached. Experience with the Allegheny Midland's stub-ended staging yards shows this to be a relatively rare occurrence, and rerailers between every other length of flextrack (fig. 9-2) usually rerail mischievous cars before major harm is done.

Visible staging can take many forms. On the

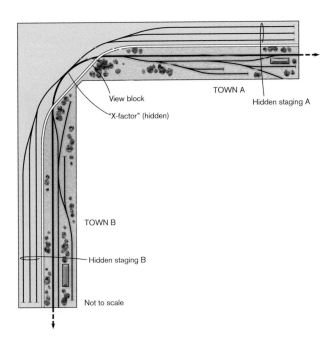

Fig. 9-6: Byron Henderson created "X-factor" staging to allow a train to head from one stub-ended staging yard back into another stub-ended staging yard via a hidden connection. After a suitable interval, it can continue its run to the other town.

Fig. 9-7: As each operating session started, this Allegheny Midland mine run was "visibly staged"—it sat on the branch waiting for its crew. It continued its run to South Fork, tied up during the day, and took empties back up the branch as the day (session) ended. This kept the branch open for other non-staged shifters to work during the day.

Allegheny Midland, some mine runs were staged on coal branches (fig. 9-7) to simulate trains returning after finishing last night's work. As the day began, they came "back down" the branch with loads of coal. As the session neared its end, the mine run took empties back up the branch. The main coal branch was originally represented by a single hidden staging track, but it later became part of the Coal Fork Extension comprising two new branches.

I also used visible staging for a local freight on an extended yard lead. As the day began, it rolled into town, thus freeing the lead for yard goat use and releasing for other service

a locomotive and caboose (assuming it wasn't assigned to a specific conductor, as was often the case during the steam and early diesel eras). As the day ended, that local went back up the branch.

Industrial sidings can be partly staged. On the AM, I put a large coal preparation plant against a wall but extended the empty-hopper delivery track through that wall onto a shelf. This let me shove 30 empties onto that track, and balance the five or six loads picked up from each of the five tracks in front of the tipple.

Another example of visible

staging on the AM was a long lead into a paper mill (visible in fig. 8-9) that allowed mill crews to switch cars destined for inside the paper mill into block order, as shown on a diagram posted on the fascia, and then shove them into that lead. The mill was theoretically out in the aisle—what I call an "aisle-side industry"—but much of the switching work was still required of the Mill Job crew.

All Sunrise, Virginia, yard

tracks and the house track past the freight house (figs. 8-7 and 9-8) were extended through an elongated hole in a stud wall onto a shelf in the adjoining crew lounge. This extended the length of the classification yard without using more railroad-room floor space and allowed more LCL (less-than-carload-lot) cars to be spotted than would have been possible if the house track ended at the wall.

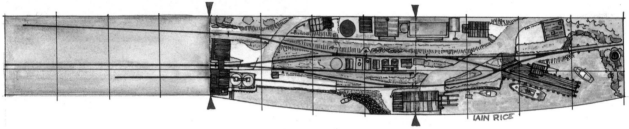

Fig. 9-8: The AM's Sunrise Yard tracks (top) continued under the through-girder road bridge onto a shelf in an adjoining room. Realism would have been enhanced by lighting and scenicking the area beyond the bridge (see fig. 9-10).

Fig. 9-9: Iain Rice used hidden tracks to extend the main line, a switching lead, and an industrial track in his Roque Bluffs plan (middle) in the October 2003 MR.

Fig. 9-10: A highway bridge (right) and, above it, a mirror hid the entrance to west-end staging on Allen McClelland's original V&O layout. The lighting and scenic backdrop enhanced realism.

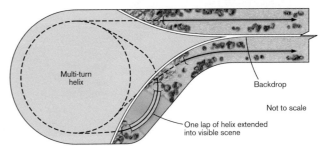

Iain Rice employed some of these ideas in his Roque Bluffs track plan (fig. 9-9) that appeared in *Model Railroader*, beginning with the October 2003 issue.

Passive staging yards can be partially modeled and partially hidden to save space, one yard doing the job of two. Allen McClelland updated the west end of the original Virginian & Ohio this way (see fig. 9-10, page 28 of *Realistic Model Railroad Operation*, and *Model Railroad Planning* 1998).

At rail-water interfaces, car floats and ferries often serve as a means to take cars across the water (fig. 9-11). Similarly, on a model railroad they can be used as platforms to move cuts between the railroad and another dock or a storage shelf. Paul Scoles explained how he used a ferry (figs. 9-1 and 9-12) on his Sn3 Pelican Bay Railway & Navigation Co. layout in *MRP* 1996.

For more information on rail-marine modeling, contact John Teichmoeller, Rail-Marine Information Group, 12107 Mount Albert Rd., Ellicott City MD 21042 (www.trainweb.org/rmig/).

Helixes

A spiral helix, which is usually hidden from view, allows trains to climb or descend between levels. However, it creates several design, construction, and operational concerns.

For starters, a helix takes up a lot of floor space unless you locate it in a turn-back curve at the end of a peninsula. A multi-turn helix to and from a staging yard or between levels of a layout also contains a surprising amount of track, causing trains to disappear for extended periods of time unless one or more turns are "herniated" out from the spiral cylinder into a visible scene (fig. 9-13).

Also, a helix may cause trains to reverse their apparent direction. A train headed to the left on one level may reappear moving to the right on the next level after moving through a helix. (Most layout designers try to keep east to the right with the "sun" at their backs.)

This may be disconcerting to crews as they try to remember which way is west or north, but it can be turned into an advantage if you need to depict a major scene from the opposite vantage point. For example, depicting a railroad that climbs along the south wall of a river canyon and crosses a bridge to the north wall can be achieved by using a helix to represent the water crossing.

The helix should not contain the railroad's ruling grade. A train that can negotiate other sections of the layout should be able to climb through the helix without stalling or needing special attention.

Last, like any long grade, a helix can be a major bottleneck. Locating passing tracks at the top and bottom of the grade, and perhaps inside the helix, will help reduce congestion.

Fig. 9-11: An Illinois Central 2-8-0 (above left) worked the Mississippi River ferry *Pelican* at Trotters Point, Mississippi. Ferries or car floats can be carried or rolled away to move cars on and off a railroad.

Fig. 9-12: Paul Scoles (top) slides the ferry *G.T. Chrey* up to the staging track apron at Port Ellerby, thus moving cars on and off "Santa Marguerita Island" on his Sn3 railroad.

Fig. 9-13: "Herniating" a helix by extending one turn out far enough for it to be scenicked lets crews check on the movement of trains up or down the helix (bottom).

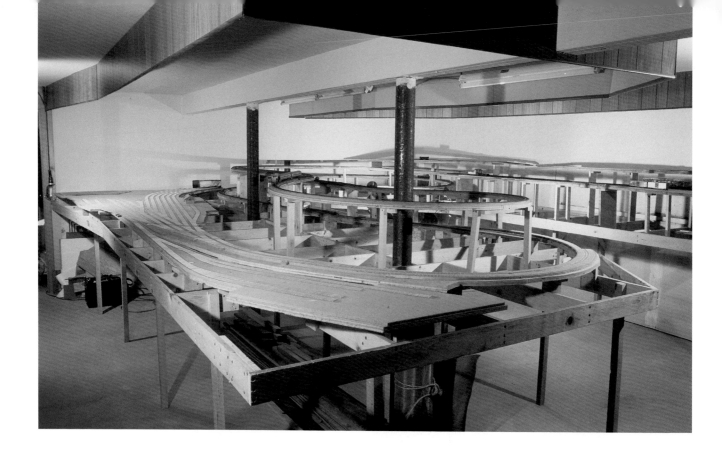

CHAPTER TEN

Construction and maintenance

Fig. 10-1: In January 1980, room prep, benchwork, and roadbed construction on the AM had progressed to this point. All benchwork was kept at the same elevation (40″) so kraft-paper drawings of the entire railroad could be unrolled atop it as a final check on track locations and reach-in distances. The higher fascias in some areas conveyed a sense of climbing into the mountains.

"If you build it, they will come"—that's a reasonable presumption for a nicely detailed model railroad that features realistic operation. But no matter how nice a layout looks, operators won't come back if you don't build it to run well. Nothing in this hobby is more frustrating than a model railroad that specializes in derailments and control-system glitches.

Fig. 10-2: Plywood shelving under the benchwork soon got in the way during layout wiring, so the shelving was used to make storage cabinets on casters.

Fig. 10-3: Commercial storage cabinets that can hold 24 years of rail magazines got a pair of 2x4 supports and casters so they could be rolled out of the way for layout construction and wiring.

Room preparation

Much as I wanted to get started on the Allegheny Midland as soon as our new home was finished, I took time to complete the layout room first (fig. 10-1). When the walls and ceiling were covered with wallboard and painted and fluorescent lighting was installed, the basement became a bright and cheery place to work. Benchwork quickly followed.

At about the same time, a friend started what would have been a nice layout in his basement but he never finished it. Instead, he got busy on a much smaller layout in a spare first-floor bedroom, and it was quickly scenicked and operating. He may have decided that he bit off more than he could chew with the larger layout, but many of his friends were willing to stop by once a week or so to help him build it. So what happened?

It was clearly the environment. With his two layouts, he had the choice of either disappearing each night into an unfinished, poorly lighted, dank basement away from his family, or staying upstairs with his wife and children in a cheery, air-conditioned area.

Another friend has built an air-conditioned barn for, among other things, his next

layout. The first floor includes a workshop, crew lounge, office, and bathroom; the layout will be constructed upstairs. He already has an operating layout, so he's holding off on this project until he retires. Then he'll substitute work on the layout for time once spent at the office, thus avoiding the need to trudge out to the barn on dark and windy nights.

Consider moving appliances and utilities before construction starts. A good time to replace an old water heater is before benchwork makes it difficult to reach. If you have an old, inefficient furnace eating up floor space,

this is as good excuse as any to buy a more efficient and compact model.

Keeping stuff off a layout can be a hassle. My solution was to build storage shelves under the railroad, but that turned into a problem when the shelves, and the stuff on them, got in the way of wiring and switch-motor installation. I converted the ¾" plywood shelving into open-front cabinets set on heavy-duty casters (fig. 10-2).

I also added casters to some commercial storage units so my magazine collection could fit under the railroad, yet be rolled out of the way during construction

and maintenance (fig. 10-3).

Good operation depends on a relatively clean environment for the railroad. An open ceiling above the railroad is an invitation to dust and hence poor operation, so covering it with inexpensive ceiling tile will pay dividends. You can also use wallboard, but it restricts access to plumbing and electrical lines. Make diagrams or take photos so you'll know where wires and pipes are located.

Carpeting, either wall-to-wall or runners along the crew aisles, will keep down the dust and add hours to the serviceability of legs and feet.

Fig. 10-4: The author made benchwork for his new HO layout from ¾″ AC-grade plywood ripped into 1 x 4s. Subroadbed is ¾″ birch plywood topped with HomaBed roadbed. Joists on risers (below) support Cayuga, Indiana, over the east-end staging yard (see fig. 9-3).

Industrial-grade 18″ carpet tiles in good condition are often replaced in office buildings, so discrete inquiries at local carpet suppliers may uncover a source for some at $1 or so per tile.

Plan fire-escape routes. Windows are often blocked or obstructed by backdrops, and a long peninsula down the center of the room may force crews to circumnavigate the railroad to reach a fire escape. Consider breakaway or pullout backdrop sections in front of windows and well-marked access openings through room dividers in the corners of the railroad room, and brief crews on their

locations and usage before every operating session. Mount fire extinguishers around the railroad and in the workshop, and check them periodically.

A foundation for the future

Building benchwork from good pine lumber, as I did for the AM in the 1970s (fig. 10-1), has become expensive and problematic. Instead, I ask my lumberyard to rip sheets of ¾″ AC-grade plywood into 3½″ strips (fig. 10-4). Those "boards" will be straighter and stronger than dimensional lumber

I join the sections with yellow carpenter's glue and sheetrock screws. Pre-drill

if you're uptight about splitting the ends of a few joists—remember, they're also glued—but the idea is to get the railroad ready to operate and not to impress the Carpentry Police.

(The same advice applies to L-girders, which can be made from ¾″ plywood "lumber." But the upper decks of multi-level layouts like the one I'm building don't lend themselves to L-girder construction, as the added thickness of the joist-supporting girders cuts down on clearances between levels.)

I make full-size drawings of track arrangements on sheets of ¾″ plywood or lengths of kraft paper

(fig. 8-8). Excess wood is cut off with a saber saw (always wear ear protection when operating noisy power tools), but I try to plan ahead by leaving the plywood intact where I intend to locate structures and roads.

I've often been asked why I cut subroadbed from ¾″ plywood. "Because I couldn't find 1″ plywood" is the truthful answer. Benchwork and subroadbed, after all, are the foundations of our railroads. Save a few bucks by buying shoddy or undersized materials and you'll pay for it over the life of the railroad. I learned the hard way that even ¾″ plywood will sag if joists

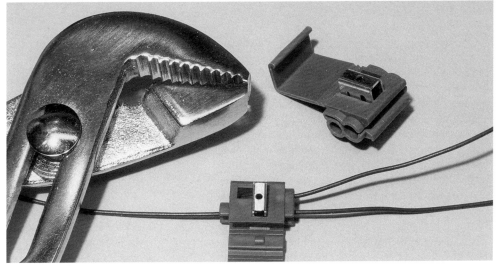

(hence lists) are spaced more than 16″ apart.

As modeler Jim Boyd observed, you can fill a gymnasium with benchwork over a long weekend. Although more elaborate planning may be needed for multi-level layouts, especially of the mushroom variety, for single-level pikes, there's not much to it. Open-grid, L-girder—just go for it! If changes are needed, fire up the power tools and make them.

Roadbed

I cover the plywood subroadbed in yards and major switching areas with ½″ Homasote sheets purchased at a lumberyard You can substitute strips of precut Homasote roadbed called HomaBed (fig. 10-4) and produced by California Roadbed Co., P.O. Box 970, French Camp CA 95231; www.homabed.com.

The ballasted main line should be about 12 scale inches higher than the sidings (fig. 10-5), which I model by using ¼″ HomaBed on the main and ⅛″ HomaBed elsewhere. I glue both types to ¼″ unbeveled HomaBed to raise the track structure another couple of scale feet above the subroadbed.

Besides deadening sound, Homasote accepts and holds track spikes better than most materials, making it ideal for handlaying track. Concerns about it expanding and contracting in moist environments are misplaced; worry instead about the much stronger plywood to which the Homasote is glued! If the railroad environment is dehumidified, the benchwork and subroadbed will stay put, and so will the Homasote.

That said, it's always a good idea to put layout-building materials in the railroad room well in advance of construction so its moisture content stabilizes. Building materials will dry out during the first winter heating season, leading to shrinkage that can cause track kinks if you haven't allowed them to get comfy in their new home. I also seal the Homasote with oil-based primer.

Allen McClelland's V&O has the quietest roadbed I have ever, well, not heard, as he cut Homasote into strips and glued them together as vertical splines. Cutting Homasote is a dusty, blade-dulling process, however, so pay a lumberyard to do it, or make a deal with your neighbor to use his table saw and garage. (Cut

Fig. 10-7: Tests on the author's 16″-wide layout showed that spacing fluorescent under-cabinet lighting fixtures even 6″ apart created dim bands on the lower deck's backdrop.

everything you'll need on the first visit, as you won't be invited back again.)

If you use commercial track components, then you have a variety of roadbed products to choose from, including Vinylbed and cork. They won't hold spikes like Homasote, but they don't have to. In *Model Railroader*, Bill Darnaby has written about using 2″-thick expanded plastic foam for subroadbed and gluing cork roadbed over it.

Using electrons creatively

Command control systems have become popular because they offer advantages—from more flexible train control to simplified wiring to remote-controlled sound—at a cost that's not much higher than installing a multi-cab DC walkaround control system. A decoder is needed in each powered locomotive, but most manufacturers now equip model locomotives with Digital Command Control-compatible wiring harnesses ("DCC ready"), or even install the decoders themselves.

Digital Command Control requires fewer wires than a comparable DC block wiring scheme. Of equal importance, the rails always

carry full voltage. This means that trying to start a locomotive doesn't involve slowly increasing the voltage between rail and wheel until—zap!—electricity arcs across the dirt that often separates the metal surfaces, creating pits in wheel and rail alike, giving dirt more places hide, and making smooth locomotive starts less likely in the future.

With command control, some current is always flowing. The increase in voltage reaching the motor takes place inside the locomotive, not at the rail-wheel interface. If crews are focused on dealing with electrical problems, they won't be thinking about realistic operation.

You also get controllable, constant-brightness headlights, which implies that crews can dim or extinguish headlights when clear of the main at a meet. And you can get sound systems, which are operationally helpful in that the horn or whistle is used to send out or recall a flagman per Rule 99 (as discussed in *Realistic Model Railroad Operation*), blow for grade crossings, acknowledge a signal, and so on.

But make no mistake;

DCC systems demand first-rate wiring practices. Signals are sent through the wires and rails, and electrically "noisy" connections or stray signals induced from parallel wires can cause trouble. Each rail should have its own drop wire and feeder to a nearby bus wire, and bus wires should be more than adequate (I use no. 10 solid) to carry the combined current loads typical of DCC systems, where many locomotives may be running simultaneously in the same electrical section.

The manufacturer of the DCC system I use recommends loosely twisting the bus wires before installation to avoid inducing voltages (signals) between parallel wires. House-current AC wiring should be kept away from layout wiring. As versatile as DCC is, I wouldn't tap power for switch motors off the DCC bus wires, as the electrical noise generated by an operating motor could interfere with digital signals.

Despite the wiring simplicity that DCC offers, it's good to break up the railroad into power districts. This reduces the current load on any one power supply, prevents one short circuit

from disrupting large parts of the railroad, and makes troubleshooting easier.

To move switch points, I use several types of slow-motion switch motors. They place little impact on the soldered joint between the switch rod ("throw bar") and points. (When I build turnouts from scratch or modify commercial turnouts to make them more "DCC friendly" by insulating the point-switch-rod and the frog, I use semi-silver solder instead of conventional electronics solder for the point-switch-rod joint. It's available at Radio Shack.)

Most types of switch motors are always powered and thus hold the point rails firmly against the adjacent stock rails. Their smooth action and low current draw almost totally eliminate turnout maintenance.

I connect wires using what electricians call "suitcases" (fig. 10-6). I used 3M connectors on the AM's Coal Fork Extension without any problems. They come in various sizes and colors; I use the red ones for small wires, and brown ones for feeder-to-bus connections. It's easier on my hand when I use a Channel-Lock type of pliers to drive home the metal

blade connector and to snap the plastic lid closed.

We tend to think of large layouts as being maintenance nightmares, but the relatively large Allegheny Midland typically required, at most, an evening of maintenance work between monthly operating sessions. I expect my new Nickel Plate to be even more rugged due to lessons learned on the AM and the use of better materials, such as ³/₄″ birch plywood for subroadbed.

When a locomotive hesitates or runs erratically, I put a 6″ strip of Rail Zip track cleaner atop both railheads and run a locomotive onto the coated section of track. With the engine running at full throttle, I hold it and move it back and forth over the treated rails. I then remove the locomotive, clean the railheads, and repeat the treatment until no trace of dirt is visible on the railhead or wheels.

Lighting

On a small layout, your lighting choices are almost unlimited. For larger layouts, however, most of us end up using fluorescent lights. My new HO layout has a 500-foot main line. If it's evenly

lighted with standard fluorescent tubes butted closely together (fig, 10-7), the total will be about 4,000 watts. But if relatively dim 60-watt incandescent bulbs were placed, say, 2 feet apart, that adds up to almost four times as much power—read "heat"—being dumped into the room.

Moreover, lighting physics shows that light from a point source (bulb) falls off with the square of the distance between the bulb and the object being lighted. But light from a linear source (tube) falls off linearly. Only a quarter of the light from a bulb 4 feet above the railroad is available to illuminate a

scene when compared to locating a bulb 2 feet above the scene; use a tube instead and you lose only half the light. Light from a "sheet" source, approximated by a multi-tube fluorescent fixture, barely falls off at typical distances.

Factor in the reddish hue from incandescent bulbs and the fact that they cast pools of light rather than linear areas of even lighting and you can see why fluorescents are the way to go. They're available in a variety of "colors," so if cool white doesn't please your eye, try something else.

Don't worry about realistic model photography when

planning layout lighting. Photography requires special floodlights and spotlights rated at the same color temperature as the special tungsten film most pros use. (Digital cameras are less demanding.) Such lighting can create sharp shadows (fig. 10-8) and other special effects.

You can have the best of both worlds with Chroma 50-type tubes, as they can be used with daylight film to produce acceptable color balance, but they look a bit too "cold" for my tastes.

What about day-night lighting effects? Dimming old fluorescents was impractical. Some of the

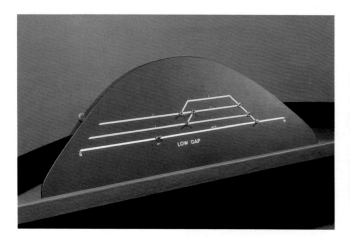

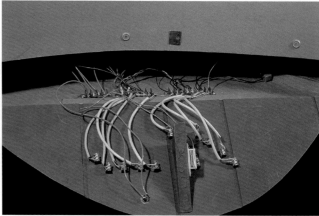

Fig. 10-9: Front and back views of the corner control panel on the author's Coal Fork Extension to the AM show simple, neat wiring that's easily achieved when block-control wiring isn't needed. The panel rests on a shelf and is secured with a magnetic latch.

Fig. 10-10: David Barrow's HO Cat Mountain & Santa Fe local panels provided track names and, across the bottom, a bar showing where the town was relative to the rest of the railroad. No electrical controls were needed, as he installed ground throws to move switch points and used command control.

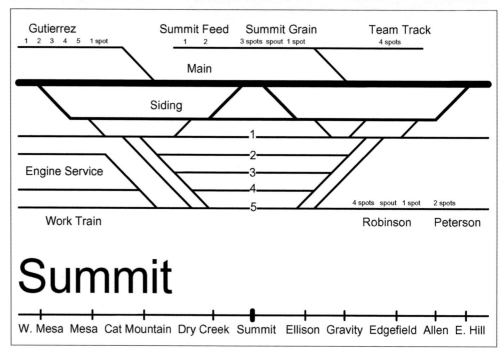

pricier new fixtures have electronic ballasts, which can be dimmed substantially but not completely without "strobing" effects. Your eyes soon adjust to the dim light, and dimmers are expensive.

My approach to daylight lighting is to use cool-white fluorescents mounted in single-tube fixtures above the upper level of the railroad Under-cabinet fixtures attached to the bottom of the upper-level benchwork light the lower level. The light levels are very bright, which is fine for aging eyes.

We've come to associate night with blue lighting, so for night operations, the fluorescents will be turned

off and a long string of parallel blue "rope" lights turned on. Incandescent building and street lights will bring populated areas to life.

One way to handle the switch to night lighting is to take a pizza break between "day" and "night" tricks and change the lighting while the crew is in the lounge. Better yet, split an operating session into 8- or 12-hour tricks, with one session conducted entirely under night lighting. Crews can carry penlights equipped with uncoupling picks, and track lighting in the aisles can illuminate work areas to facilitate reading the paperwork.

To ensure that I didn't

overload existing AC circuits with railroad day and night lighting, I had an electrician install a branch panel just for the railroad. Everything can be shut off at one central point when I walk out of the basement. Leaving a soldering iron plugged in under the railroad could literally light up my life.

Control panels and fascias

The days of the central operating pit with its theater-size control panel for the maestro to attend to are thankfully behind us. It was hard to get to such pits or to reach anything else once the operator was ensconced. Modern layout design calls

for linear, walkaround plans with every effort made to avoid low duckunders.

As we walk along with our trains, we need to be able to reach the controls without having to race back to a central panel. Put another way, crewmembers shouldn't have to stand far away from their trains just so they can be near the control panel.

An easy way to accomplish such goals is to use walkaround or, better yet, wireless (radio or infrared) command control, which precludes the need for block toggles or rotary switches. When hand-thrown switch stands are also employed, there's no need to ask

Fig. 10-11: John Breau's attractive crew lounge has callboards for his Great Northern Butte Div. and foreign-road crews. There's plenty of room for off-duty crews to sit down away from the action, but—appropriately—those seats don't look too comfortable! Chuck Hitchcock photo.

another person or use panel lights to tell whether a switch is lined correctly; everyone will be right there where the action is.

For those of us who like to use switch motors, the question of where to put the controlling toggle switch arises. Small local panels are a good solution (fig. 10-9). They can contain helpful information, such as direction arrows and perhaps a schematic showing where you are, and which towns are nearby, as David Barrow did on his Cat Mountain & Santa Fe (fig. 10-10).

Another approach is to use model aircraft striping tape to create track schematics on the fascia, with each turnout control located in line with the switch points. DCC can also be used to activate switch motors using a handheld throttle, but some sort of switch labeling system is still needed so an operator will know which address to call up.

Those with conventional DC systems can avoid the "Who's got my train?" hassles with a simple procedure. Have each engineer set all block control toggles or

rotaries to power his or her cab to the clearance limit given by the dispatcher prior to moving the train. If the dispatcher says a train is cleared from Frankfort to the passing track at Wingate, its engineer sets all the controls between those two points to his or her cab, including aligning the switch into the siding and setting the siding block control at Wingate.

Since the engineer has an oral or written clearance, he or she owns that part of the railroad, so all the block controls should be set up in advance. That way, a train won't accidentally run into a block still connected to someone else's throttle. The engineer doesn't have to kill blocks behind a train, as whoever gets clearance into that block next—such as the train being met—is obligated to set everything up within his or her clearance limits before moving on.

Crew lounge

If off-duty crews don't have a convenient lounge (fig. 10-11), they will imitate relatives during the holidays, who invariably gather in the kitchen, by standing in the

most congested aisles and talking to the busiest guy on the railroad.

A well-equipped crew lounge will include amenities such as a small fridge, coffeepot and hot water for tea, a sink, and a nearby toilet (to preclude having crew members traipse through family space to reach the bathroom.

But don't make it too nice or you'll find it difficult to pry crew members out of their comfy chairs to fill the next job assignment.

Workbench area

I'll wager that most of us would make more progress on our layouts if we did our modeling in more pleasant surroundings. A cold garage, dim basement, or hot attic isn't going to entice us out of the TV room.

This also applies to the workbench area. Joe Crea, who is well known for his large-scale modeling, moved his workbench into the living room to be closer to his family. This required a change to water-based paints to avoid harmful fumes and nasty odors, and he created

a work space that was both attractive and easy to cover up between work sessions.

My list of improvements planned for my own workbench area includes cable TV so I can keep up with favorite programs without losing too much modeling time, a stereo, a telephone, and perhaps an Internet connection.

I've installed lots of cool-white fluorescent lighting around my workbench and painting area, which is the same lighting used on the railroad. This ensures that a model's perceived color won't shift between the workbench and the railroad.

Getting things done

Back in the 1970s, when I was the editor of *Railroad Model Craftsman*, Dave Frary and Bob Hayden did most of the product reviews for the Test Track section. I asked them how they got so much modeling done, as both had full-time day jobs. Dave said he got up an hour early each morning and devoted that time to modeling. For nightowls, an hour before dinner or bedtime may work better.

CHAPTER ELEVEN

Crews and jobs

Fig. 11-1: Getting together for an operating session, even outdoors on a live-steam system, is fun and educational, yet challenging. It also motivates progress, as you know that the crew will drop by soon to see what you've been working on since the last session.

It's possible to build and operate a model railroad alone, but sharing it with others on a regular basis can be rewarding. Such cooperative efforts range from taking field trips to gather information and participating in work sessions to sharing hobby knowledge and operating the railroad (fig. 11-1). Moreover, progress is typically much more rapid when friends contribute to the railroad on a regular basis. Scheduling regular work or, as soon as practical, operating sessions virtually ensures continuing progress.

Fig. 11-2: Harold Werthwein is building an enormous HO edition of the Erie's Delaware Division that features many large "signature" scenes and structures, such as this sprawling brick depot in Susquehanna, Pennsylvania. In return for providing a place for Erie fans to operate, he expects them to work on the railroad between sessions.

Fig. 11-3: The author's goal is to re-create the action he witnessed in his hometown in the mid-1950s (right), including having an operator-towerman work the NKP-C&EI interlocking plant at Cayuga, Ind. Photo courtesy Charlotte Miller.

Group dynamics

The work session host should identify tasks for each person or team of people to perform. If everyone is busy with an assigned task, fewer disagreements on the "best" way to accomplish a given job will arise.

There are almost always several excellent solutions to a given problem. Each of us tend to embrace the one that has worked for us. Those individuals with a mechanical bent may prefer to use manual linkages to move switch points, for example, whereas those think electrical devices provide a more elegant movements will lean that way.

Your role as the project manager may be to ensure a demarcation exists between assigned tasks. Remind friends that yours is not a club layout—you as the owner appreciate their help but do have clear objectives. As long as you can articulate those objectives and keep everyone focused, disagreements will tend to be minor and short-lived.

Some layout owners take a strong stand about work versus play. Those who show up to help build the railroad are the same folks who get first choice of jobs during operating sessions. A local modeler has made it clear that he expects regular operators to help with specific construction projects, including building key structures, because his layout is too large for him to do everything (fig. 11-2).

I tend to work alone. A couple of close friends volunteered to help, but I find that coordinating my schedule with theirs is not practical. Moreover, before they arrive, I have to define jobs for them and make sure needed tools and materials are on hand, which is a lot like doing project management for a living.

But the times we managed to get together, we made progress and had a lot of laughs. Moreover, creative ideas came out of our problem-solving discussions that would not have occurred to me working alone.

When to operate?

Choosing a convenient time for work or operating sessions can be problematic. Before I retired from my 9-to-5 job, weekends were precious and I didn't want to use them for operating sessions. Therefore, I picked the fourth Friday evening of the month, assuming that attendees could sleep in the next morning. "But I have a 6 a.m. tee time at the golf course," complained one operator. "I work Saturdays," said another.

A local modeler schedules one of his two monthly sessions on a Friday evening and the other on a Saturday to accommodate most. Still another has found that sessions beginning late Sunday morning work out best for his crew. I've also heard about weeknight sessions, but as Paul Dolkos observed, "Weeknights seem not to work as well, as people begin to tire early and want to cut and run."

New horizons

Now that the idea of learning the art of operating a railroad by timetable and train orders has established a beachhead in the hobby, the role of the telegraph operator is being expanded. Most operators in small towns were also the railroad's freight agent. As far as the fellow who owned the local grain elevator or lumberyard was concerned, the agent was the railroad.

Before the "day" (session) begins, the agent-operator makes his or her rounds to see what work will need to be done at the towns along his or her section of the railroad. The agent can see from the waybills that a couple of boxcars are loaded with grain at the Thompson elevator, for example, so he can anticipate a need for a pair of clean, empty boxcars suitable for grain loading.

A list of such needs is made up and called in to the yard, where today's local will originate, so enough empties (MTYs) can be switched into the local to meet the needs of customers on this part of the division. When the local arrives at each town, the agent meets the crew there to help them spot the MTYs.

timetable and the freight schedules book (fig. 11-5) for that period, and I can compare actual experience to management goals by looking at dispatchers' train sheets or employee time books (fig. 2-9).

How do I know the NKP offered enough action to keep several crewmembers and me busy? Here's where benchmarking becomes important. Finding another layout that's similar to the one you plan to build can be helpful. Thanks to magazine articles, layout tours during hobby conventions, and Internet chat groups, that's not hard to do.

Don't just sit there . . . .

You've persisted through 11 chapters of facts, figures, personal opinions, examples, how-to suggestions, the occasional poke in the ribs, and even exhortations. I'll close with one of the latter.

I've spent the better part of a full and highly rewarding lifetime learning about model and prototype railroading. This book was conceived as means to passing along as much of it as I could squeeze between the covers.

Now it's your turn: Find a way to use this information to make progress on your existing or planned model railroad. As Dave Frary observed, an hour a day can do wonders. Learn as you go, have a lot of fun along the way, and make every effort to share what you've learned with another generation of modelers.

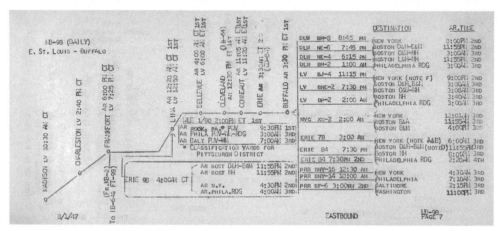

Fig. 11-5: Keeping everyone focused on a common goal is easier when you have a prototype's example to follow. This page from the NKP's 1954 freight schedules book documents the operation of MB-98, which will run over the author's new layout. This information will help yardmasters block this train.

Such jobs aren't going to attract the "I just wanna run a train" crowd, but there are ways around such concerns. Not everyone has to do every job, although in my view this is not the best approach. I'd rather rotate all crews into most jobs so they familiarize themselves with the duties yet aren't stuck there for the entire session. Some members will never like jobs that don't involve running trains and switching cars, but many will find that such assignments are more interesting than expected.

Controlling evolution

John Swanson wrote eloquently in *Railroad Model Craftsman* about how his freelanced circa 1923 HO granger railroad evolved to meet the needs of almost everyone who had a suggestion about how the railroad could be operated.

Both John and I came to the conclusion that we had lost control of our railroads.

We both made major changes as a result. John completely redesigned his Dixon, Wyanet & Lake Superior. My objectives had changed so drastically that I abandoned the railroad and built a new one based on a favorite prototype that embraced timetable and train-order operation.

Keeping expectations realistic is easier for me now. My job is to learn as much as possible about how that part of the NKP operated in 1954 and to provide a platform for that to be re-created in HO scale. I have the employee